W9-AJM-082

LADIES AND GENTLEMEN— START YOUR VACUUMS

Admit it. No one—except for your mother-in-law, and you know she's lying—really *loves* to clean. But there is help! This never gritty guide gives the lowdown on the best way to clean up, making most unwelcome chores practically painless. Inside, you'll find the answers to such housecleaning problems as:

- How to safely clean TVs and stereos
- Getting paint specks off a window
- The pros and cons of Scotchgard
- Cleaning behind appliances and heavy furniture
- Attacking even the grungiest bathroom tile, and more

Filled with first-rate advice from America's top expert in commercial cleaning, *Do I Dust or Vacuum First?* shows you how to make a clean sweep of things and earn more time for yourself.

DO I DUST OR VACUUM FIRST?

Ⓜ MENTOR   Ⓟ PLUME   Ⓢ SIGNET   (0451)

FOR YOUR INFORMATION

☐ **READY FOR TAKE-OFF:** *The Complete Passenger Guide to Safer, Smarter, Air Travel* by Marie Hodge and Jeff Blyskal. Discover simple steps to protect yourself from air crashes, unsafe airlines and terrorists; learn the secret of getting first-rate service—for cut-rate fares; learn how *not* to get bumped—and how to get generously compensated if you do, and much more! It's the no-nonsense traveler's lifeline! (169352—$3.99)

☐ **DON ASLETT'S STAINBUSTER'S BIBLE.** From acids to Kool-Aid to mildew, this uproariously funny book tells you how to zap even the most stubborn stains from all surfaces, including silk, leather, synthetic fabrics—and even white things! This guide will prove invaluable to anyone who knows how to spill. (263859—$9.95)

☐ **THE REAL ESTATE BOOK by Robert L. Nesson. Revised edition.** A complete guide to real estate investment including information on the latest tax laws, mortgage tables, and a glossary of terms. "Indispensable"—*Forbes* Magazine (155203—$4.95)

Prices slightly higher in Canada

Buy them at your local bookstore or use this convenient coupon for ordering.

NEW AMERICAN LIBRARY
P.O. Box 999 – Dept. #17109
Bergenfield, New Jersey 07621

Please send me the books I have checked above.
I am enclosing $_____ (please add $2.00 to cover postage and handling). Send check or money order (no cash or C.O.D.'s) or charge by Mastercard or VISA (with a $15.00 minimum). Prices and numbers are subject to change without notice.

Card #_____ Exp. Date _____
Signature_____
Name_____
Address_____
City _____ State _____ Zip Code _____
For faster service when ordering by credit card call **1-800-253-6476**
Allow a minimum of 4-6 weeks for delivery. This offer is subject to change without notice.

Other Books by Don Aslett

Is There Life After Housework?

Clutter's Last Stand

Who Says It's a Woman's Job to Clean?

Make Your House Do the Housework

Pet Clean-Up Made Easy

Cleaning Up for a Living

Is There a Speech Inside You?

How Do I Clean the Moosehead?

Don Aslett's Stainbuster's Bible

Not for Packrats Only

500 Terrific Ideas for Cleaning Everything

Don Aslett's Clean in a Minute

VACUUM
FIRST?

**AND 99 OTHER NITTY-GRITTY
HOUSECLEANING QUESTIONS**

Don Aslett

EAU CLAIRE DISTRICT LIBRARY

A SIGNET BOOK

87525

SIGNET
Published by the Penguin Group
Penguin Books USA Inc., 375 Hudson Street,
New York, New York 10014, U.S.A.
Penguin Books Ltd, 27 Wrights Lane,
London W8 5TZ, England
Penguin Books Australia Ltd, Ringwood,
Victoria, Australia
Penguin Books Canada Ltd, 10 Alcorn Avenue,
Toronto, Ontario, Canada M4V 3B2
Penguin Books (N.Z.) Ltd, 182–190 Wairau Road,
Auckland 10, New Zealand

Penguin Books Ltd, Registered Offices:
Harmondsworth, Middlesex, England

Published by Signet, an imprint of New American Library, a division of
Penguin Books USA Inc. This is an authorized reprint of a hardcover edition published by writer's Digest Books.

First Signet Printing, March, 1993
10 9 8 7 6 5 4 3 2 1

Copyright © 1982 by Don A. Aslett
All rights reserved. For information address Writer's Digest Books, 1507
Dana Avenue, Cincinnati, OH 45207.

REGISTERED TRADEMARK—MARCA REGISTRADA

Printed in the United States of America

Without limiting the rights under copyright reserved above, no part of this
publication may be reproduced, stored in or introduced into a retrieval
system, or transmitted, in any form, or by any means (electronic, mechani-
cal, photocopying, recording, or otherwise), without the prior written per-
mission of both the copyright owner and the above publisher of this book.

BOOKS ARE AVAILABLE AT QUANTITY DISCOUNTS WHEN USED TO PROMOTE PROD-
UCTS OR SERVICES. FOR INFORMATION PLEASE WRITE TO PREMIUM MARKETING DI-
VISION, PENGUIN BOOKS USA INC., 375 HUDSON STREET, NEW YORK, NEW YORK
10014.

If you purchased this book without a cover you should be aware that this
book is stolen property. It was reported as "unsold and destroyed" to the
publisher and neither the author nor the publisher has received any pay-
ment for this "stripped book."

Thanks to the key players in this cleaning adventure, 112,261 homefront folks, Judith Holmes Clarke (mother of seven) for super illustrations and Carol Cartaino "thee" editor of fifteen of my books!

DON ASLETT,
WHY DOES EVERYONE
ASK *YOU* THE
CLEANING QUESTIONS?

After thirty-five years of cleaning homes and businesses I realize there are situations that have no simple, neat, "revolutionary" answer. There are some real stumpers, to which the answer is just what you thought—i.e., it's a tough, tedious job, and there's no magic tip, no presto super-duper solution: "How do you clean feather pillows? . . . What is a *FAST* way to clean ovens? . . . How can I clean a cottage-cheese ceiling? . . . How can I get my kids to clean up their rooms? . . . How do you fold fitted sheets neatly?" These are problems to which there is no easy, comforting answer—but there *is* an answer to most cleaning problems, I assure you! Even if the answer has to be "Have a professional do it," or "Destroy it and buy a new one." Lack of knowledge to solve a cleaning challenge is not the big problem: lack of ambition, nerve, or money to proceed is usually what leaves a cleaning mystery unsolved.

I cleaned thousands of homes professionally in ten years of working my way through school (Idaho State University). And for the last twenty-five years I've handled cleaning problems in thousands more homes—plus millions of square feet of commercial buildings—across the U.S.A. I've raised six children (and had six teenagers at once!) and faced all the real-life challenges a home cleaner does. And I now head one of the major cleaning firms in the country. Some people call me the best, *America's #1 Expert* on cleaning. Well, I do know a lot and have done a lot, but there are hundreds of you who know how to do certain things better and faster than I do. (When you analyze "expert" you realize that "X" is an unknown quantity and "spurt" is a drip under pressure.) Though I've tried to answer even the toughest questions as fully as possible, my answers aren't the end of the line—the final word—there will be a better answer someday! But please, though I'm not the be-all and end-all of household wisdom, read these answers with an open mind (all the way to the end!) and you may well learn something truly helpful (if only what *not* to do). Be aware, too, that techniques and approaches to specific cleaning problems can often be applied to very different cleaning situations, so be alert as well as open.

I've gathered the questions in this book from all the homemakers I've met in my travels, my professional work, and my personal life. At the housecleaning seminars I give across the country, every day new questions come. In choosing 100 to include in the book, we've selected not only the ones we thought the average homemaker most needs the answer to, but also questions it's practically impossible to find an answer to anywhere else. We included a few questions that we wouldn't have otherwise, simply because they're asked so often. And we even threw in a few "rhetorical" questions to help boost your morale in the never ending war on dirt.

If you have a burning question not addressed in these pages, please do send it to me so I can be sure to consider it for the *next* edition: Don Aslett's Cleaning Center, P.O. Box 39, Pocatello, ID 83204.

SHOULD I DUST
OR VACUUM FIRST?

First, if you mat all entrances, inside and out, you'll cut dusting and vacuuming in half (see page 104). Once your matting is down, always *DUST FIRST!*

Boo! Hiss! Snort! Argue! "If I dust first, then vacuum, it blows dust on everything I've dusted," says Vera Vacleak, Dust Bowl, Arizona. If your vacuum is in that bad a shape you're wasting your time dusting *or* vacuuming. A good vacuum with a decent bag and clamps won't leak and spew dust over cleaned surfaces. When you can *see* "resident dust" (it causes that dusty/burny smell when you turn your vacuum on) as well as smell it, you know your filter's not good. A vacuum has to be maintained. Dump (or change) that bag at least once a year. (I'm kidding, of course.) Seriously, if you empty or change the bag frequently you'll spend a *little* time emptying instead of a *lot* of time wondering why the vacuum isn't picking up like it used to.

Dusting is more than picking up minute particles of lint or airborne residue on a picture frame. *Dusting* is scraping dirt and dead flies off window sills; wiping up eraser rubbings and food crumbs that missed the napkin; getting all the ashes, orange and apple seeds, gum wrappers, and fingernail clippings off the living room furniture, as well as the toothpick ends cleverly hidden around the lamp by the easy chair; knocking mouse droppings off the drapes. If you vacuum first, all this ugly litter ends up on your freshly vacuumed floor. (Ugh!)

I've heard a lot of Vacuum-Firsters argue that even a good clean well-filtered vacuum blows dust and dirt off undusted or forgotten areas onto dusted ones. Well, get *rid* of undusted or forgotten areas— use your imagination. Close in that dusty area, or find a way to rig your duster to get it. Remember to pick up and capture the dust, not spread it around. Masslinn dustcloths and lambswool dusters do a great job of this and nail the dust.

HOW DO I GET BLACK MARKS
OFF THE WALL?

EAU CLAIRE DISTRICT LIBRARY

13

Black marks generally fall into the categories of *"art-work"* (felt markers, crayons, pencils), *"club" marks* (from broom handles and baseball bats), *"rub" marks* (from chair backs and furniture too close to the wall), *"lean" marks* (from things like skis and mops) and *"bumps"* (from furniture and acts of everyday living—even—gasp—carelessly wielded vacuums).

Don't overestimate the size of a mark and make a headlong dash to remove it at all cost. Too many times, a tiny black mark on a nice enamel wall causes the homemaker to go into hysterics and—as she's learned from the latest "Helpful Hint" book—grab some toothpaste or peanut butter and rub not only the black mark, but the whole general area. Both of these "agents" do much more than take out black marks. They are abrasives and will leave a large dull spot that's usually more noticeable than the original mark. (Besides, peanut butter is too expensive to clean with!)

What is the right way to get rid of black marks? First (after you've hidden all the felt-tip markers), examine the mark and determine if it is removable. Most markers on a good varnished or gloss surface will come off. But remember that felt-tip marker dyes vary so much in their chemical makeup that there is no one magic remover. Sometimes markers stain; sometimes the ink just lies on the surface. If the mark is in a natural untreated wood or other porous surface, it's probably stained and all the rubbing and scrubbing you can manage won't touch it.

If it seems to be cleanable, dip a corner of a clean cotton terry cloth in a solution of neutral cleaner (see p. 242) and rub *the mark only*—not a six-inch-square area—with the tip of your finger behind the cloth, the object being not to damage the paint finish or surface. Press harder as you go; this should take most of it off, then buff with a dry part of the cloth. If only a slight shadow remains, I'd leave it. If you think the mark will bother you more than a tiny dull area, dip the wet cloth in a little abrasive cleanser and rub lightly just on the exact area of the mark—this will take out the mark and only a little of the surface.

If the spot doesn't appear to be cleanable, touch it up with the leftover paint you saved in a baby food jar. Use a little artist's brush and feather the edges out. It will stand out like a sore thumb at first, but in a short time it will blend in.

If the problem spot is on wallpaper, glue a piece of paper from your leftover roll over it (slightly larger than the spot and congruent to the closest pattern). Few observers will ever detect it.

When it comes to marks, face the fact that if you have children, grandchildren, or neighbors who are a constant threat, you must provide a wall surface that can be cleaned. Flat paint, elaborate fabric wall-covering, wallpaper, unfinished wood and the like are always going to come off badly from a tangle with markers. Eggshell enamel, plastic laminated paneling, and sealed wood surfaces all resist spot and stain penetration and are much easier to keep looking sharp.

HOW DO I CLEAN CHROME AND KEEP IT LOOKING GOOD?

Chrome is an easy surface to clean, but often looks bad when you're finished because a dull surface will absorb the light instead of reflect it. The secret is to use a dry cloth to give it a final polish after you clean it. Most people use either a damp rag or an oily one, and because of chrome's intense reflective quality, every smear is exaggerated. A soft dry cloth will buff, polish, and brighten the freshly cleaned surface up nicely. I minimize chrome surfaces in my house, but wherever it lurks, use an evaporating alcohol-based glass cleaner (such as Windex) and polish with a dry cloth. If the surface is greasy, clean it first with a hand dish washing liquid solution.

The way to keep chrome looking good is to keep it dry and dusted, or every little particle and print will show. (If this sounds impossible, it probably is.) It also helps to clean chrome more often than every six years, so scum and hard water deposits don't have a chance to build up. A little mild phosphoric acid cleaner will get off any hard water deposits that have accumulated—rinse the surface after cleaning, then dry it shiny.

WHAT'S THE BEST WAY TO GET RID OF COBWEBS? IS THERE ANY WAY TO PREVENT THEM?

A lightly oil-treated* dustmop or a damp towel on the broom will pick up the webs most efficiently. A web will cling to damp surfaces and can thus be gathered, instead of being knocked loose and allowed to float onto something else.

A well-known exterminator remarked to me, "I've never seen a house that was spider- or mouse-proof." It's almost impossible to keep spiders out. They migrate into the house (generally through cracks in the foundation and house base plates—where the house attaches to the foundation) and once in they usually like it. A consistent spray program around the base of the exterior foundation will work if you want to spend the money. Or you could seal every crack and tiny hole in your dwelling.

Pick your cobwebs when fresh, and it will go easy and fast. If you let them hang, fine coats of grease will settle on them and magnify the problem.

*Commercial dustmop treatment preparations can be purchased at a janitorial supply store (see pp. 175–76).

WHAT IS THE BEST AND EASIEST WAY TO CLEAN MY VENETIAN OR MINI BLINDS?

The easiest way *is* the best! But before I share my wisdom, let me share a bit of history. From the fifties to the mid-sixties, venetian blinds were a big part of my cleaning list and schedules, home and commercial. I invented a massive machine that failed, visited car washes (they do a bad job), and tried the bathtub caper (which most homemakers use). I was always cleaning more of me than the blind. The old cotton glove trick was terribly slow and sloppy. Around 1965 (because no one knew how or wanted to clean them?) blinds seemed to disappear! Between 1967 and 1975 I cleaned or was called to clean nary a louvered shade, so I dismissed it as a forgotten art.

But like every clothing style we struggle with, the venetian blind is back—in a scaled-down version, the mini-blind—but still, because of the horizontal slat design and the fact that they're located at a window, blinds get dirty fast with that same sticky stuff that gets on top of the fridge! Cleaning a slat at a time while the apparatus is in place is slave labor, and generally does a streaky-poor job. Again, car washes won't clean them well, and if you've tried the bathtub you know that's not the easiest or best method. For regular maintenance of blinds, I'd dry-dust them with a lambswool duster (see p. 244). By closing the louvers you can dust a flat area instead of cleaning them slat by slat.

After a year or so you find blinds sticky, fly-specked, and coated with a film of dirt. It's time to clean them. *First*, do them ALL at one time. *Second*, adjust the blind to wide-open (so the most light can come through), then pull the blind all the way to the top, release the fastener clamps, and remove the blind unit from the window mount. (Be sure to wrap the cords around the blind so they won't drop or get ripped or caught during handling.) Find a hard surface, preferably slanted and preferably outside—such as a concrete driveway or patio. Lay an old carpet or thick quilt of canvas on top of it. You need something soft like this to lay the blinds on so they won't scar. Open the blinds, hold at the top, and adjust the blind slats to the utmost vertical position (so they lie flat). Flop the blinds on the cover now. Take a soft-bristled brush (I always cut an old floor push broom in half), dip it in ammonia solution, and scrub, getting back under the ribbons. The first side will come clean in a few seconds. Reverse the blind (by turning it completely over so the other side of all the cleaned slats is showing), then scrub this side. Use a *little* powdered cleanser (which will have a bleaching and mild abrasive action) on the ribbons if they don't look clean. Your padding material (carpet or quilt) is now saturated with water and cleaning solution and will keep the opposite side moist and help clean it. When both sides are clean, carefully hang the blind on a ladder or clothesline (or have someone hold it) while you rinse it with the hose, shake it once or twice to help prevent water spots, and let it dry.

This may sound a little awkward, if not barbaric, to do, but I assure you it isn't. I can clean blinds six times faster than any other method this way, leaving them grease- and film-free.

Levolor blinds (a modern version of the horizontal-slat venetian blind) are coming more and more into style. If you have them, clean them like venetian blinds (it'll help you remember why venetian blinds went out of style—they're a maintenance nightmare). Vertical Levolor or venetian blinds don't catch dirt or grease and stay clean longer.

WHAT DO I DO ABOUT A DIRTY ACOUSTICAL TILE CEILING?

You have, as of a few years ago, two good alternatives (to replacement) for acoustical tile ceilings—even walls. My favorite is the dry sponge. A dry sponge is a flat rubber pad that acts as an eraser and actually absorbs dirt from the surface when rubbed across acoustical tile. It is extremely fast and unmessy. You should be able to get dry sponges at paint or hardware stores (if you can't, write me at P.O. Box 39, Pocatello, ID 83204 and I'll give you a source). Acoustical tile can be easily and permanently damaged beyond most ordinary cleaning means by the combination of oils, grease, cigarette smoke, water leak stains, and the sags and tears that come with time. Eventually, because of the tile's absorbent quality, even a dry sponge won't do much good.

When tile is in tough shape, the final alternative is to paint it. Painting, of course, will improve the overall appearance and offer a better surface for future cleaning. The bad news is that painting retards the acoustic value (and the acoustics are generally the reason the tile was installed in the first place); it also gobs in the cracks and the design or print, sometimes making it look a little tacky.

Because soiled tile is and has been a big problem in commercial cleaning some people recently figured out a way to "oxidate" or renew the surface without using paint; we have used this system successfully in our commercial buildings. Soil on acoustical ceilings is of three general types, each of which is removed separately:

1. Dirt and soot—especially around heating and cooling vents.
2. Yellow-brown material—residue and tars from tobacco smoke and cooking exhausts.
3. Stains from water soaking through the ceiling.

During the cleaning process, the loosely adhering dirt and soot are removed by brushing and vacuuming. The cleaning solution, which is sprayed on, contains a variety of ingredients, each of which attacks a particular component of the ceiling soil. Where does the dirt go when the ceiling cleaning solution is applied? It doesn't disappear as if by magic; rather, the dirt, having had its physical properties changed by the chemical, loosens and falls to the dropcloth. The cleaning chemical will also loosen dirt on fixtures and grid supports and they can be wiped down.

A similar approach to this was used a few years ago, with a bleach spray; it did a fairly good job, but the mist could cause chemical pneumonia and the ceiling smelled like a swimming pool afterwards. If you have a lot of tile in your house, apartment, or business, consult your Yellow Pages for a local source of chemicals or assistance. The method should be duck soup easy in a home. Follow directions— and be sure to cover up everything—and you will be impressed. If damaged or stained spots remain, feather over them with a little flat white latex paint.

But try the dry sponge first. It's easier!

WHAT IS THE FASTEST, EASIEST WAY TO CLEAN LIGHT FIXTURES?

Before starting, make sure the light is off and cooled. Unscrew mounts or fasteners. This will allow you to take down the lens and put the mounts back on the screws or bolts (nothing is worse than trying to find a tiny lost mount or digging one out of the goose-neck of your sink drain).

Either soak the lens in a sink full of hot soapy water, or wet it down with a sponge of soapy water and leave it on the counter. (You're letting it soak—just like a frying pan you've let go a few days.) The residue on light fixtures, especially those close to the kitchen, is tough to get off—airborne grease, cook-ing and cigarette smoke, bugs and flyspecks that have been baked on by the lamp bulb's heat. If you have the patience to let the lens soak so the sticky stuff will dissolve, the job will be easy. If instead you scrub the unit, your chances of scratching the design or breaking the lens are good. Let it soak until the dirt releases, then rinse it with hot water and let it drip dry. I've seen light fixture specifica-tions that say not to wipe the lens with a cloth be-cause it leaves a static charge that attracts more dirt.

If you need to wash a fluorescent lamp bulb, take it out or wear goggles—I've seen too many bulbs explode or break above heads when bumped, show-ering eyes with glass, sodium, and bits of metal.

Lampshades (the bane of the living room cleaner) can easily be cleaned with a dry sponge (see p. 24). And you can clean any chrome, brass, tin, or pewter that may be part of a lamp unit with a spray bottle of evaporating alcohol-based cleaning solution (like Windex). To return the metal to its original luster, you might even use a little metal polish!

P.S. I'm sure glad you didn't ask me about chandeliers!

HOW DO I CLEAN CRAYON AND CEMENT-HARD FOOD OUT OF HEAT VENTS?

You've probably got some hard wax, mop strings, spider webs, and antique lollipops or Life Savers in there, too. Grubby heat vents (floor or wall units) look terrible and are hard to clean and unhealthy— I feel better just knowing yours will be clean.

Don't try to clean them in place—it's too messy and will take too long. Ninety percent of floor heat vents can be slipped out; others might require removing one or two screws. Pull them out and take them to a central cleaning location. Fill a sink (or preferably, a five-gallon bucket) with hot water and mix in wax stripper or a heavy-duty cleaner and let them soak. Most of the dirt will be released and can be knocked off with a light scrub-brushing; if you scrub them violently, you'll strip off too much of the enameled finish (then they'll look tacky and will rust). Be sure to flex the "louver mover" (if there is one). Rinse the vents and let them drip dry.

If they're getting beat up over the years, line them up someday (after a good cleaning) and give them a coat of good hard enamel spray paint.

DO YOU THINK IF I GLUED MY DOG'S HAIR TO ITS BODY I'D HAVE LESS TO CLEAN UP?

Animal "fallout" (shedding hair/fur) on floors, furniture, clothes, and car interiors is a problem many people are stuck with. The best cure is to keep the animal outside. The next best is a good beater brush on your vacuum—hair has little "lift," so plain attachment tools without a beater brush are slow and ineffective. The revolving brush will help lift the hair/fur from the surface; once detached from the rug, upholstery, or clothes surface it can be vacuumed more effectively.

The next move is to get a "pet rake" (see p. 245)—this is a hand brush that looks like a thin push broom. The crimpled bristles are constructed to do a good job of gathering the animal evidence to a central location, then you can dustpan or vacuum it up. The tape rollers made for lint removal, or packing tape wrapped around your hand does a good job on small areas like clothing.

Hair doesn't stick to hard-surface floors, walls, and furniture, so it can easily be picked up with a damp cloth or a dustcloth.

When it comes to carpet, high pile "hides" hair better than low.

Glueing your pet to one spot might also be a good idea.

WHAT ABOUT THOSE WHITE RINGS ON FURNITURE WHERE A GLASS OR CUP SAT?

I suggest you drink at the sink—there's no doubt those rings are ugly and tough to get out! Don't let anyone convince you there is *one* miracle way to get them out. It's complicated because there are at least forty possible combinations of circumstance that could have caused the mark: the furniture material itself, the furniture finish, the polishes or waxes used on that finish, the amount of heat and light (such as the ultraviolet of sunlight) the finish is exposed to, etc., as well as the length of time the object remained on the spot. For example, the heat from a coffee cup resting on certain lacquer tops causes a chemical change in the lacquer, or a cold drink may cause a chemical reaction between the polish and finish—the result in either case will be a ring mark.

Strangely enough, most of the time if you leave the ring alone, the light and temperature of the room will cause the surface to "heal" itself. (A little prayer may help, too.) Light rubbing with pumice, 000 steel wool, or a gentle abrasive compound may get rid of it, but that's risky, depending on the finish. Don't rub polished furniture with a dry abrasive or it will dull or scratch the rubbed spot—dampen the area with a little lemon oil, water, oil-based lubricant, etc. (Whatever you use, be careful—go slowly. Woods and finishes vary so much I can't give you a specific method.) If you still have a problem, I'd wash the surface with a mild neutral cleaner solution, dry it with a cloth or towel, and wait a few days. If it doesn't go away try rubbing it with a little furniture polish, or call a local wood refinisher. . . .

HOW CAN I CLEAN BEHIND AND UNDER APPLIANCES AND HEAVY FURNITURE?

Areas behind, under, over, in back of, are generally non-depreciable surfaces—in other words, dust, grease, and grime isn't hurting anything if it stays, as long as you can't see or smell it. Of course, knowing the dirt is there (whether it's visible or not) makes it almost "immoral" not to clean it (plus the problematical fact that those areas can provide excellent reproductive environments for germs, bugs, flies, mice and their relatives). And too much of a dust and debris buildup around belts, motors, and pilot lights can be a fire hazard.

First, use good judgment. Vacuuming is almost impossible, unless you've got a flat two-foot long "hypodermic" vacuum attachment. (If you do any vacuuming behind an appliance, unplug it first! Dinging around with a damp cloth in back of electric appliances can disassociate you from any more worries, if you hit an electrical short or happen to "ground.") Several commercial brush manufacturers make a yard-stick-looking radiator brush. This is great to get the fur and dust: it can get down the side, under, and back of most appliances.

If you must pull an appliance out to clean behind it, remember these items are also heavy and awkward for even the biggest and huskiest of us, and one bad drag or pull can gouge a permanent mark in walls, floors, or furniture. Some appliances have short cords or pipe attachments that restrict manipulation, so don't yank something loose. If you have to pull an appliance out and it has no casters, always lift the front and set the bearing points of the legs on a thick doubled towel or anything else that will slide easily and not mar the floor.

WHAT ARE THE MOST DREADED AND FAVORITE HOUSEWORK TASKS?

Judging from the calls, letters, and comments I've had from the hundreds of thousands of people (mostly women) I've taught in my seminars, homemakers are always interested in expressing their feelings on this subject and finding out how others feel about certain household jobs. I've received a lot of input on "favorite" and "most dreaded" housecleaning work from the comment cards I pass out. After sitting down and computing the input, this is what I've found:

Favorite:
(After turning on the dishwasher, hiring a maid, and getting through)
The Number One: (almost three times as popular as Number Two) *Vacuuming*.
The Number Two: *Dusting and polishing*.
The Number Three: *Washing clothes*.

Most Dreaded:
(This list was much more lengthy and opinionated)
In the Number One slot we find: *Bathrooms*. The average homemaker dreads bathrooms three times as much as she does dishes.
The close second was: *Windows*.
A steady third: *Ovens*.
And a close fourth: *Dishes*.

I don't know if these statistics offer any comfort (it might help to know you have company in your hidden housework feelings—both joy and misery love company).

WHAT ABOUT NO-WAX FLOORS?

A no wax floor is about like a no-wash dish! A recent full-page ad in a popular national women's magazine promoted a floor that "shines without waxing." On the very next page of the magazine was another full-page ad that said in bold print, "IS YOUR NO-WAX FLOOR GETTING DULL? Mop and Shine brings no-wax floors back to life beautifully." In smaller print the ad continued, "No-wax floors are great, but in time, even the best no-wax floor can start to lose its shine. Household traffic can wear down the toughest finish, and detergents can leave a dulling film." I agree with the last sentence: the extra-thick protective clear layer on top of these is great and means a very shiny finish when new, but the "no-wax" label is misleading. They aren't going to look good indefinitely. Sand, grit, particles of broken glass, etc., which adhere to or embed in footwear, will be carried inside and abrade and damage any surface that doesn't have a protective coating. The urethane-type finish used on a no-wax floor will perhaps last a little longer than the finish on a regular floor, but wear will eventually dull it. Dullness is not only a loss of the reflective finish, it generally means wear is now grinding away on the floor material itself, not just the finish.

To investigate the claim that no-wax-type floors do not need protective maintenance (wax) to retain their original gloss, a chemical manufacturer's association ran an eight-week study, simulating the traffic of 80,000 human steps. Findings showed that no-wax floors do have a high original gloss that holds longer than an ordinary vinyl—but that without periodic applications of a protective finish *any* floor dulls, wears, and becomes more difficult to clean.

Many floor dressings are much like whitewashing a fence—they improve the looks, but do little protecting. Instead of "dressing," keep your floor coated with a good polymer floor finish. Wax heavily in heavy traffic areas, but to avoid wax buildup don't overdo it on the edges of the floor, under the furniture, or other little-used places. Do this and you can accurately rename your "no-wax" floor a "no-wear" floor.

HOW DO I GET THAT STICKY, GREASY DUST OFF THE TOP OF THE REFRIGERATOR?

Elementary! Spray on a hand dishwashing liquid solution (about 10 to 1 with water) or a solution of heavy-duty cleaner (see p. 45), let it sit on there a little while to break down the greasy film, then wipe it off. If it rolls off in little balls, it means you've waited too long to clean it and the chemical action of your soap or detergent can't handle the thickness. Clean it more often and it will wipe off much easier and quicker. If the stuff is *really scummy*, use a disposable cloth or paper towel for the first wipe.

HOW GOOD ARE THOSE HAND CARPET SWEEPERS?

A carpet sweeper is a non-electric hand-powered tool that looks like an anemic upright vacuum. With a pass or two over the surface, it can whisk litter from the carpet or floor. You're going to hate me for this next sentence . . . but carpet sweepers are like girdles: they can make the surface look pretty good, but don't help a bit with the real problem. Because sweepers are fast and easy to use, people who have them have a tendency to use them only—and neglect their good beater vacuum, which removes the soil, sand, pencil lead, crumbs and the like from the depths of the pile. The result is excessive deterioration of the rug from unseen debris below the surface. If carpet sweepers are only used occasionally or for emergencies (like scooping up scattered popcorn between shows or cleaning Cheerios off the carpet before company arrives), they're great and I could endorse them, but being a realist, I avoid any temptation to give the carpet too many "once over lightlys!" (And I don't think such infrequent use justifies the extra tool.) Sure hate to split up that love affair!

Q16

WHICH CLEANER IS BEST?

First, don't lose too much sleep over this question. There isn't enough difference in most cleaners to really matter. Rip, Snort, Sizzle, and Guzzle are all essentially similar. The basic elements in most cleaners are *alkalis* (such as caustic soda, lye, soda ash), *surfactants* (less phosphates these days, other more environmentally safe substitutes), and *sulfates* (such as anionic sodium salts). Different manufacturers use modified phosphate-free or other special material, but this must be balanced with yet other ingredients in order to do a good job of cleaning—and all the formulas end up very much alike. Most cleaners are a sick yellow-brown color when formulated— they usually have a dye added to differentiate them from Brand X and to make them look appealing.

Americans are brand fanatics, hypnotized by the colors and jingles and bursting soap bubbles of TV commercials. If I said get "El Snort" cleaner and someone couldn't get that brand conveniently, they'd row the Amazon to find it. We all have strong feelings about our favorites but most of us couldn't tell one from the other.

For example, there are at least 30 good 35mm cameras on the market. If I took 30 pictures, one from each camera, the average person couldn't tell the $169 from the $1,200 product. So it is with cleaning products—be true to *types*, not brands.

On most products, if you get the right *type*, you're okay, as most soaps, heavy-duty cleaners, all-purpose cleaners, etc., are so similar few of us could distinguish one from another. Concentrated disinfectant cleaner, for example, is a type of product of which many brands are available, all very much alike in chemical composition. Some work a little better than others, but it's not worth the time or emotional strain to find the "perfect" one.

If you want to make life simpler, I'd advise you to have only three types of cleaners:

1. *A neutral all-purpose cleaner.* "Neutral" means a cleaner that's right in the middle between the 0–7 pH of acids and the 7–14 pH of alkalis.
2. *A disinfectant cleaner* for bathrooms and other areas that need germ and odor control. Check the label—"quaternary" is the kind you want.
3. *An evaporating alcohol-based window cleaner* for little windows: you squeegee the big ones (see *Is There Life After Housework?*, p. 45). This is also great for polishing chrome and other "bright work" in the house.

I'd buy all of these in concentrate form at a janitorial supply store (see pp. 175–76), either in jugs or in premeasured packets. Buy 3 one-quart trigger spray bottles and use your own water and the *right* amount of concentrate (not "a little extra to be sure it works good"). If you buy from a reputable place the cleaner will be as good as or even better than the supermarket variety and 75% cheaper.

We'll see the day when a homemaker can bring a 6-month supply of cleaners home in a purse or lunch pail. A great percentage of what you carry out of the supermarket is water; it costs plenty to package, ship, and store water.

Products and compounds are no magic, only your tools for the application of intelligent cleaning techniques. I use a few brand names—like 3M, for example—they put out good stuff, it's expensive, but lasts and works better than most of the competitors' similar products. I also like Eureka vacuums for their design, price, and durability. One squeegee I don't think can be matched is the Ettore, but other commercial brands work.

HOW DO YOU CLEAN UP HAIR IN THE BATHROOM?

Great question. It's asked by 10,000 motel maids and 788,520 homemakers every day. The good news is that this hairy cleaning chore isn't that tough. A clean, damp, textured cloth (such as a washcloth) will pick hair off tub, counter, and sink surfaces easily. The trouble is, the hair on the cloth can then easily be caught or snagged by any rough surface, and as the cloth dries a little the hair will be redistributed on other areas. Using the same cloth to clean the whole bathroom is ineffective and yet it's inefficient to use several cloths.

Professional cleaners and smart homemakers can dehair a bathroom in a second. They grab a couple of tissues or a few squares of toilet paper, and dampen part of it slightly (not to the point of disintegration). Hairs are generally in "flow" areas of tubs, sinks, and counters, and a few swipes with the damp tissue will remove them. (Don't worry about mini-hairs from shaving; they just flush right down the sink, and unless your drain is badly clogged they won't get caught.) Toss the tissue in the wastebasket and then proceed with your regular bathroom cleaning.

Here's something else that will help the problem: install a mirror in an open area away from the sink. This encourages hair care to be practiced *away* from the sink. (Hair is less alarming on the floor or rug because a vacuum beater bar can deal with it.) Have you ever pulled out the drain stopper in your sink or tub? Then you won't have to wonder why water goes down the sink so slowly—the stopper will be absolutely hanging with matted hair and soap gunk. Stoppers should be cleaned every month. Most units can be pulled from the top without tools.

WHERE DO YOU START IN A CLOSET?

Listen to an old "Fibber McGee and Molly" tape—there's always the part where Fibber opens his closet and in a great 30-second burst of sound effects all the crammed-in junk pours out. Radio listeners loved this because it was familiar (just like home). In twenty-five years on the air Fibber never learned—but you can.

1. You start in a closet by *dejunking* it. That is the simple (and often heartrending) process of getting rid of everything you don't use or need. We all know what *is* junk and what isn't. Dresses, pants, shirts, and shoes that haven't fit or pleased you for the last twelve years won't ever—pitch them! Those hand-painted ties and leopardskin clutch bags aren't coming back in style: pitch them. Those boxes of Christmas cards from 1978, 1979, 1980, 1981, complete with address lists: face the fact that you'll never write them . . . burn them. Etc., etc.

That's Principle Number One: DEJUNK YOUR CLOSET. Once this is done, the restorative process is simple.

2. Move the useful but used-once-a-year (or every 2–5 years) stuff to a less critical (inactive) storage area. Remember, closets are your most accessible active storage area. Attics, under the basement steps, or basement storage rooms are not, so transfer the worthwhile but not-fre-

quently-used stuff (like camping gear, out-of-season clothes, scuba-diving masks, suitcases, etc.) to other areas.

3. *Get stuff off the floor.* Floor mess is about the most psychologically devastating of all messes. Most closets have a lot of unused upper room—for a few dollars worth of material and a spare hour or two and you can install (or barter with a friend to install) a second shelf above the one over the hanger rack.

4. If you are a person who rotates shoes, clothes, or gadgets for "sanitation" or style, there are pocketed wall or closet organizers you'll find useful. Just use your head in choosing—and installing—"storage organizers." Some are real helps; and others just help you store junk higher and deeper.

5. I realize most of us don't have enough closet space—but don't pack too much into your closets. You'll defeat the purpose. No matter how cleverly you fit it all in, and alphabetize and "organize" it—if a system won't stand up to quick, convenient use, it's ultimately doomed and will aggravate the mess. Overcrowding makes it a lot tougher both to get things out and put them away!

6. Use hard-finish, light-colored enamel when you paint, and hanger marks can easily be cleaned off.

7. Relax—closets don't need to be cleaned as often as the rest of the house because they are essentially concealed storage, not a public area even to the family, so there is some excuse for having your closet any way you like. Maybe Fibber enjoyed the avalanche of junk!

AMMONIA—SHOULD I USE SUDSY, "LEMON-SCENTED," PLAIN, OR . . . ?

It doesn't matter. As long as it smells like ammonia and shrivels up your hands, it's okay! I generally use plain (colorless) ammonia. Stick to supermarket ammonia—it's inexpensive and packaged in a safer dilution and more convenient container for household use. Commercial establishments sell "commercial" ammonia in a stronger dilution ratio. That scares me because ammonia users are often in the habit of taking a big whiff before they use it (to make sure it is indeed ammonia) and the concentrated fumes of commercial ammonia are dangerous. Household ammonia requires no complicated conversions to use, you just add water.

Ammonia is great to clean many things with—but two warnings:

1. Bleach, when mixed or used with ammonia, will create a deadly gas.
2. Ammonia, if left sitting too long on a surface, will bleach or spot (your car finish, piano top, hardwood floor, etc.) because when water begins to evaporate out of a 20 to 1 diluted water/ammonia solution, it becomes 15 to 1—10 to 1—5 to 1—and soon it is straight stuff!

Ammonia cleans okay because it's alkaline on the pH scale and cuts grease, but now there are lots of "as-good-as, less smelly" cleaners out there!

MY FLOOR HAS A DESIGN WITH HUNDREDS OF LITTLE INDENTATIONS, WHICH ARE FULL OF WAX AND DIRT. WHAT DO YOU THINK?

I think it's the "pits!" That's kind of like asking how to clean the ground, because old wax buildup and accumulated crud are below the surface and there's not much you can do to get it out. Even powerful scrubbing machines glide over these indentations without doing much good. If your cleaner or wax stripper is working right (commercial strippers are best), it will soften and emulsify the contents of the "pits" so if you mop and rinse with enough water, much of the problem will float out and you can pick it up. But you do have to depend on dissolving, not scrubbing, action to get it out.

Two other choices, as long as it's all evenly dark: leave it that way—few people will notice! Or if it *really* demoralizes you, replace it—most floors can be replaced for a few hundred bucks.

P.S. Somebody also ought to replace the engineers who are sadistic enough to design dirt traps in a modern floor!

HOW DO I CLEAN GREASE SPOTS IN BACK OF THE STOVE?

Those grease bumps grow so hard that even the toughest dissolver can't work up enough action to loosen them, and they're so slick that most pads, cloths, and brushes just slide over them. Use a Choreboy type (curly strand) metal scrubber with a good degreaser, such as a heavy-duty cleaner. The little sharp metal edges will easily cut into even the hardest grease, and won't hurt the surface as long as it's good and wet with cleaning solution. Be sure to let the cleaner soften the grease awhile before you start to scrub—and wash your metal scrubber right away to get the grease out while it's soft.

HOW DO YOU CLEAN A KITCHEN EXHAUST FAN?

Dread-inspiring as they may be, hanging there covered with grease and dust, exhaust fans and other kitchen circulation vents are not difficult to clean. Most of them are removable, and the first thing to do is to unscrew or unstrap the cover plate, then take it off and immerse it in a sink full of hot water and strong grease cutter (dish soap, ammonia, or wax stripper, etc.). Now leave those parts to soak and look up into the exhaust opening; you'll see a grease-laden motor with a fan blade also heavy with sticky fuzzy grease. This unit is small and light and comes out easily—first reach in and unplug the cord, then lift the unit out of its little motor mount and set it on some newspaper on the counter or table. Wipe the heavy grease off with a disposable cloth or heavy paper toweling, then spray it with your squirt bottle of heavy-duty cleaner solution and polish it up. (Be careful not to wet the exposed windings and other electrical parts of the motor.) Get back up on your five-foot step ladder (the ideal size for inside work), wipe out the now unobstructed opening, and spray and polish it, too. (By the way, this is a great safety measure; it goes a long way toward preventing grease fires.)

Put the clean motor and fan unit back in the mount, plug it in, and test it by switching it on; it should work perfectly. Now go to the sink and clean the cover grill or vent that has been soaking; the solution should have released most of the grease, so it will be easy to finish up. Dry, polish, and put it back in place.

The procedure for vented range hoods is similar, except that most of the motors will not be removable. Let the grease-trap filter soak while you clean the hood, then spray it out with steaming hot water. Replace the charcoal filter or non-vented units as necessary.

I've cleaned hundreds and hundreds of kitchen fans/vents; believe it or not, they only take ten to fifteen minutes. Try it—you'll be so proud of yourself when you're finished that you'll take the rest of the day off.

HOW DO I GET THE STAINS OUT OF THE BOTTOM OF MY TUB?

The yellow ("rust") stains you are probably referring to are also found in the bottoms of sinks, showers, and sometimes old toilets. They are generally caused by water dripping or standing for long periods of time. If they've been there many a year, you won't get them out—the minerals in the water have removed the enamel or porcelain finish and actually permeated the glaze. Harsh cleansers and bleaches and other oxidizers will whack it away a little, but will leave the area so porous as to stain up faster the next time. Commercial rust remover, however, will often remove the yellow stain—follow the directions on the can including all the safety precautions.

Any dripping water, of course, must be stopped. Oftentimes a 25¢ faucet washer will cure the problem. Showers, tubs, sinks, and toilets susceptible to this problem should be cleaned regularly with a diluted phosphoric acid solution like Showers N Stuff (see p. 245) to keep minerals from "setting up."

If the stain is just soap scum or hard water residue, a phosphoric acid cleaner applied with a white nylon scrub pad will take it right off.

THE "ROUTINE" (SAME OLD THING EVERY DAY) OF HOUSEWORK REALLY GETS ME— HOW CAN I BREAK IT?

The "routine" syndrome afflicts almost anyone doing anything (school, art, acting, travel, romance, fishing, skiing, and writing can all become as routine as housework)! We get up at the same time, eat the same breakfast, drive the same car down the same road past the same scenery. We work in the same place, and although individual situations and the people we have to deal with are different from day to day, we basically do the same thing with them, in the same way. It's hard to get around this, having the same experience fifty times is simply not as fulfilling, interesting, or motivating as having fifty different experiences.

The answer is finding a way to turn your routine (common) experiences into uncommon, challenging ones. I think the home offers more opportunity for this than any other work environment. Here's what I do; maybe it will give you some ideas.

1. *Compete* with yourself to cut the time a routine thing takes to do. Even "fun" jobs are dull and boring if they take forever; the quicker and more cleverly we can do them, the better off we are. (Like trying to find a different, faster route home.) Things, no matter how common, that we do faster and better than anyone else turn us on and leave the routine "drags" behind.

2. *Eliminate* the routine jobs that weren't necessary in the first place (like ironing socks, folding underwear, setting a second fork, spraying

pine scent, putting on fake eyelashes, washing the car twice a week, etc.).

3. *Delegate* the fun stuff. Remember how many now-routine chores were once fun (getting the mail, shopping, buying and sending gifts, polishing, making a special dessert, driving, etc.)? Now that you've done them for twenty years the fun is long gone. You have a family, friends, enterprising neighbors, youth organizations, and professional associates, who could enjoy and personally benefit from some of these chores, so let *them* have them. I give most of my routine work away now—and most of the receivers who end up doing it find it challenging and refreshing because it's *new* for them.

4. *Make a change.* Americans work to "have it made"—to find a place and position where our lives and emotions will never again be threatened and we can live in security and ease. "Ease," defined, is simply routine, and eventually that's the very thing we end up hating! Environmental changes always bring new experiences, pressures, challenges, relationships, curiosity, risk—and this I promise will solve the "routine blues." Try a change in your habits, work setting, associates—just remember that the change doesn't have to be *radical* (like leaving home, getting a divorce, hitchhiking around the world, taking a lover, or joining a militant group). I've seen small things like new bedspreads, visitors, taking up a new sport, going back to school, even a new time to get up in the morning, greatly change a routine—and a life.

HOW DO I GET GUM OUT OF A CARPET?

Go to a janitorial supply store and get a little can of "freon freeze." Spray it on the gum—this makes it brittle, and it can then be shattered into tiny pieces that will release from the carpet. Gather or vacuum up the pieces immediately before they soften and compound the problem. The remaining residue can be removed with dry-cleaning fluid. If there's still a spot, rub it a little with a clean damp towel wrung out in neutral cleaner solution.

A little can of freon will last a long time and save you hours of grief. Ice in a plastic bag or dry ice can also "brittle-ize" the gum enough to shatter it, but it's slower and messier.

I also use a citrus-based product called De-Solv-it that works on gummy labels as well.

Because I'm a cleaner and I've seen those nasty little globs cost companies and schools hundreds of thousands of dollars, I've come to feel that gum chewing is ill-mannered. If I caught a person leaving gum in my carpet, I would quickly remove the person who deposited it there.

DON, WHAT'S THE FIRST THING YOU NOTICE WHEN YOU WALK INTO SOMEONE'S HOME?

I start before I get in, looking for the doormat. If there is none (or only a tiny rubber thing that trumpets the owner's name), I wince and prepare myself for the dirt in the house! I *know* dirt is in there (see p. 104), so I don't have to look for any.

The first thing I notice as I *enter* a home is how used and livable it looks and feels. I'm more impressed by that than by a perfect, expensive, plushly decorated showplace. Is the music out on the piano—because it's played—or tucked neatly into a bench with an unused polished seat? I'd rather see a cookie jar with a few crumbs around it than a gleaming sterile tile counter top. The smell of warm fudge, fresh baked cookies or bread, clean wash, or hobby glue sure beats the aroma of "air fresh'ner." Stains from canning fruit on a sink are a plus, not a minus, to me! A HOUSE IS MADE TO *LIVE IN* NOT LIVE FOR!

I notice wall decorations, too—I like to see family crafts and pictures—a John Van Smear original (if Johnny lives there) impresses me more than a Van Gogh. Dust always looks worse on pretentious store-bought trinkets—miniature ships, kewpie dolls, coats of arms, and eagle plaques—than on family things. Next I listen for the concert of human interaction, young, old, and middle years—and the harmony of the music it makes.

All of these things I notice before the "cleaning" details—but have no doubt, I do get around to the physical conditions—and in the negative sense that this question is usually asked, I have three top candidates:

Number 1: *Clutter, litter and junk* is a big part of what I notice in a home. I can accept enough dust on the coffee table to write "welcome," but I can't forget that order costs nothing (and ridding yourself of litter and junk can even help you *make* money). Disorder and mindless accumulation not only tarnish the image of a home and its occupants—they give me the unhappy message that the inhabitants are "out of control," oppressed by their surroundings rather than served and comforted by them.

Number 2: *Wax buildup* is next. I can't hack dark yellow edges on a floor. It's easy to avoid this (as I explained in detail in *Is There Life After Housework*) by always remembering to wax heavy on traffic areas and *light* under furniture and in corners.

Number 3 *The basic condition of the dwelling*—it pains me to see chipped and peeling paint, walls that reflect abuse and lack of maintenance, not normal wear.

For some reason, cobwebs don't bother me—they can spring up (spin up?) overnight. And you can stop worrying—dead leaves on plants (on the floor or in the pot) don't bother me either.

P.S. But don't worry, since I've become a "world famous housecleaner," no one invites me home any more.

WHAT SHOULD I DUST WITH?

First, you shouldn't be dusting much. Probably 80% of dust comes in on and is moved around by people, so mat your doors (see p. 104). I'd also check weather stripping, clean or change furnace filters, and vacuum regularly, and there won't *be* much dust. Second, cheap feather dusters and oil-soaked rags are out. They create more problems than the original dust—rinky-dink feather dusters and blower attachments on a vacuum just move the dust around, and oily rags leave a sticky surface to attract and hold dust. Real ostrich feather dusters, however, work great! Professional dustcloths, called Masslinn cloths (though they're really paper), permeated with a tiny bit of "dust treat," are pretty good. So are the electrostatic dustcloths such as the New Pig. Ledges, door tops, beams, wooden shelf tops, etc., are often rough and will catch and snag your cloths, so I'd recommend you un-rough the areas with a light sanding and a coat of urethane finish, varnish, paint, or whatever matches the existing surface.

The fastest, most effective light dusting in high places is done with a big wool puff (it looks just like cotton candy on a stick). You can get these at janitorial supply stores. They're called lambswool dusters and are made of real lamb's wool. They catch and hold dust by static electricity, and do a super job on uneven surfaces like moldings and blinds, too.

A lightly water-dampened cloth is an okay dust collector for the tops of window sills, rails, or shelves. If the cloth gets too loaded then it will leave wet dust that comes back to life when it dries! Remember, your object is to pick up the dust, not to knock it from one place to another, and not to leave an oily film that will attract and hold future dirt and dust.

71

ARE OLD OR NEW HOMES
EASIER TO CLEAN?

Modern building codes, engineering, design, and materials put new homes way out in front for ease of cleaning. The average new home has 8-foot ceilings; old homes have 9- and 10-footers. Woodwork and baseboard trim in new homes is plainly designed and the edges are slanted, so that dust rolls off; in old homes it's wide and often decorated with mitered grooves and flat edges that catch dust and dead flies. Windows in old homes (often jalousie or small-paned) are much more difficult to clean and maintain (and for that matter, to open); a modern house has thermo single-slide units. Open heat and old-fashioned furnaces are often thought of as dirtier than modern units, but the real culprit is the lack of insulation in old houses: poorly insulated outside walls make inside walls get filthy faster.

Old homes need old-style furniture to complement them, and while an 1892 maple rolltop desk is beautiful and worth $2,600, it is a cleaning/maintenance nightmare, compared to a $260 built-in desk and file in a new home. Hardware is a great time-taker in cleaning; old homes have more! Doors in new homes—mahogany, birch, or plastic—are generally flat, smooth, and simple in design; in old homes their embossed or carved decorative trim is a pain to clean *or* refinish. The walls and woodwork of old homes have usually been painted so often that they look a little "gobby" and saggy, even when clean.

Flooring quality and installation techniques have

improved tremendously in the past thirty years; floors in new homes are far less of a cleaning challenge. Man-made fibers in modern carpet are more easily maintained than the old cottons and wools. Cellars and attics, common in old homes, weren't exactly an assist to cleaning efficiency (mainly because they offer uninhibited junk storage) and dirt floors in cellars were accepted in even the finer old homes.

Bathroom fixtures in old homes are tougher than the new plastic and fiberglass styles, but they've endured years of "grinding" with scouring cleansers that has deteriorated the surface—making cleaning harder.

All in all new houses are easier and faster to clean and keep clean. The only problem is the average new home is much bigger (and fuller of junk), so in terms of time it's almost a toss-up. (Of course "new" is automatically expected to be cleaner, so you owners of old homes can get away with more!)

I HAVE STAINLESS STEEL SINKS AND APPLIANCES, AND I CAN'T MAKE THEM LOOK GOOD.

It might make you feel better to realize that stain-less steel isn't *non-staining* steel—it stains *less* than plain old steel, but it does stain and it's not your fault. Stainless steel lasts, doesn't rot or rust, so it has a nice claim as a good surface!

First: Don't get overly excited, and quit swearing that you're going to paint all the stainless steel in your house! Stainless steel, especially the brushed surface found on most sinks or kitchen appliances, will soon cloud, streak, and water-spot, and slowly take on a permanent "used" look. In other words, it stains! In some of my commercial buildings I have 600 stainless steel drinking fountains to clean. They are a high-complaint item, hard to clean—and once clean, they deteriorate quickly.

A lot of elbow-flexing will leave the unit pretty decent, but generally after a dribble of anything on it, the glowing surface looks the same as before you started.

I personally wouldn't *have* stainless steel in a glamour place in a house. Get vitreous china or por-celain fixtures for easier cleaning.

If you do have stainless steel:

1. Clean it thoroughly with a mild detergent solu-tion, rinse, and buff it dry with a cloth or towel.
2. Some "house prouds" treat stainless steel ap-pliance panels, etc., with lemon oil, waxes, silicone-type materials, or other protectors for a nice luster or "glow." It looks good, but re-member, in the long run any treated surface will require more upkeep.
3. Some commercial aerosol stainless steel cleaner/ polish formulations work well (3M is one of the good ones).

WHAT IS THE BEST WAY TO CLEAN RUGS?

The best carpet cleaner by far is a combination of effective matting to keep soil out (see page 104) and good regular vacuuming with a beater brush or bar-equipped machine to remove any soil that does get in. Eighty percent of carpet soil comes in by foot traffic, and good mats at the entrances will keep a great deal of it from ever getting onto the carpeting. Add regular vacuuming with a good beater type vacuum to your matting program, and you will vastly reduce the amount of deep cleaning your carpet will require.

When your carpet does reach the point where it needs to be cleaned, first consider having it done by a professional. He or she will have the equipment and expertise needed to get out all the deeply embedded soil that damages carpet, and to take care of special stain removal problems. Rental units don't have the power to do a good job, and most homemakers don't have the know-how or the chemicals they need to accomplish a really good deep cleaning on their carpeting.

The best method to ask for is a combination of rotary shampoo on heavily soiled areas and hot water (steam) extraction overall, with pre-spraying where necessary. After your carpet is cleaned, or when you first have it put down, I also strongly recommend the application of a good soil retardant (3M's Carpet Protector is one) to help your carpet shed soil and stains and extend the time between major cleanings. A professionally deep-cleaned and soil-protected carpet will look nice for a long time with nothing more than the simple maintenance described earlier and occasional spot cleaning.

If you still insist on getting the rental unit from the supermarket and doing your own, you want to know which kind of shampoo or steam cleaning solution is best, right? There are so many brands available, it would be impossible to list them all, but you can make your own simple test. Most of the products do an acceptable job of cleaning, the big difference is in the type of residue they leave. Put a little of the shampoo you intend to use in a flat dish and let it dry out thoroughly. Some shampoos will leave a brittle, powdery residue that will vacuum out of your carpet easily and not attract new soil. Others leave a sticky or gummy residue that coats the carpet fibers and accelerates re-soiling. When a freshly cleaned carpet re-soils quickly, it's most likely because a sticky soap residue was left after cleaning.

WHAT SHOULD I DO WITH MY WOOD SURFACES?

Not what you are led to believe! All kinds of oils, conditioners, lemon formulas, grain groomers, and other concoctions are foisted on unsuspecting home-makers as "good for wood." Most wood surfaces (walls, paneling, floors, furniture) have a coat or two of a clear resinous finish over them that seals off the actual surface of the wood and presents a varnish or plastic finish—it doesn't allow any of this "miracle" wood stuff to get to the wood anyway, so you can use the same diluted cleaners on your wood that you use to clean other surfaces.

No special procedure is needed to clean wood that has a sealed finish. I've even used wax stripper on my birch cupboards—it dissolves the kitchen grease/oil in seconds and doesn't hurt the wood because it doesn't ever *get* to the wood. On paneling, I always use a solution of oil soap, such as Wood Wash, Murphy's Oil Soap or the new Pledge wood soap. Note, I said *soap*—I use Murphy's not because the finish needs to be oiled but because Murphy's has enough vegetable oil to make the panels shine up when cleaned and buffed, which saves application of the spray gunk polishes. Harsher cleaners won't pro-mote a nice sheen.

I don't really know how to clean bare wood. If it is smoke-stained, greased, or crayoned, cleaning generally makes it worse. If moisture gets into wood, it swells the grain and accelerates deteriora-tion, and if the wood has paint or finish on it, the swelling will eventually chip off the finish. So it isn't wise to wet your wood down (most of you know that, thus the miracle wood oils are sought). If you want to keep bare or raw wood around (if you *want* to suffer), it may need to have a penetrating oil such as lemon oil applied *periodically* from time to time to keep it from drying out.

Wood surfaces are nice in a home; they project homey warmth, but when you plan them, make them maintainable. Wood that keeps you so busy cleaning and treating that you don't have time to appreciate it is stupid! (All the knots aren't in the wood!)

I think feeding wood (walls, furniture, or the like) is a ridiculous waste of effort and material. Finishes are available that seal the surface, and if applied right form a glass-like membrane over the wood. That beautiful grain will still be bright and clear and fully visible, but marks and stains end up on the membrane instead of in the wood. Use a satin or low-luster finish.

If you wish to apply or reapply a varnish or membrane coat on ailing wood surfaces:

1. First, clean the surface with a strong cleaning solution (a strong ammonia solution, wax stripper, or degreaser if it's a surface that's previously been sealed; solvent if it's raw wood) to remove dirt and grease.
2. Let it dry until any swelled wood grain goes down.
3. Wipe with a deglosser. This can be bought at a paint store; follow the directions on the can.
4. A few strokes of superfine sandpaper will take care of any bumps.
5. Then wipe with a cloth dampened with paint thinner (or a tack cloth) to pick up any lint or dust on the surface.
6. Apply the finish (paying attention to the *directions*), it may take two coats.

If you have any other questions, consult a good local paint store.

HOW CAN I ENJOY MY FIREPLACE WITHOUT ICKY SOOT AND ASHES?

I've had fireplaces in all my homes—in fact, I designed and built them myself, thinking of course that I could always heat my house with them after the enemy captured all the oilfields, and the A-bomb cut off all electricity. When I learned that most fireplaces pull heat *out* of the house instead of putting it in, I converted the open hearth to a metal insert (a wood- or coal-burning stove that fits neatly inside the fireplace). I had a warmer house, but still had soot and ashes.

At the American Booksellers Association convention one year I met Dee and David Stoll, famous professional chimney sweeps (they were the ones married atop the Sears Tower). I found out that chimney sweeping is a serious and necessary business: if your heating unit, be it a stove, fireplace, or whatever, is working well, soot and ash will be minimized. I've seen properly installed carousel fireplace units burn for weeks—they were so efficient only a few handfuls of ash remained.

In time creosote and soot will accumulate in any chimney, greatly reducing its efficiency, increasing the chances of getting dirt and smoke through your house, and making you susceptible to a dangerous chimney fire. Clean your chimney, then check the dampers (see that the opening and closing mechanism works). That's the easiest way to get "de-ickee-d." There are many professional chimney sweeps available; however, make sure they are certified to inspect as well as to clean. If you are an adept roof scaler and want to do it yourself, you can purchase chimney rods and brushes (they come with directions). Be sure to seal off the bottom before you start or you'll have icky ashes all over your house!

Leave the damper open when scooping up ashes and soot, and most dust will go up the chimney instead of all over the house.

Make sure ashes are "out" before vacuuming them or tossing them in the trash.

ANY TIME-SAVING IDEAS FOR CLEANING KNICKKNACK SHELVES?

Anything full of "things" (or out of reach) takes longer to clean—that is a fact of housecleaning. If you only keep the things you really love enough to dust and clean regularly, you'll eliminate most of the knickknacks on high shelves (maybe the little kids can't reach them now, but *you* can't see or appreciate them much either).

Alas, there is no simple answer to the knickknack question—because there are 2,200,723,857 different fuzzy, prickly, shiny, sparkly, metallic, dull, pasty, glossy, waxy, etc. knickknacks in existence. Many are cheap souvenirs, and they seem prone to damageable surfaces. Even some of the sturdier stuff that won't snag or break easily will often discolor when water touches it, or crumble or fade from cleaning operations. In one house I cleaned after a fire (smoke damage), would you believe 7,400 knickknacks? They were of good quality and we hand-cleaned them in a sink, like dishes. Grease-laden washable knickknacks benefit from wiping/washing lightly with hand dishwashing liquid.

Overall, on knickknacks I use an ostrich feather duster. If I'm going to handle them I choose a Masslinn cloth, a soft treated disposable commercial dustcloth that picks up dust and dirt and leaves the surface clean, or an electrostatic dust cloth, or even a lambswool duster depending on how much room I've got to cover. If you don't have any of these, use a damp cotton cloth. On a large rough-textured surface, a vacuum with a brush dusting attachment is hard to beat (as long as you keep a firm grip on the knickknack in question).

The biggest timesaver, if you are a knickknack addict, is to enclose the little charmers so they can be seen and enjoyed without worries about settling kitchen grease, cobwebs, flyspecks, and *dust*. "Enclosing" usually means a glass cover in front of the shelves—or buy a china cabinet.

A little hard thinking on your part will save a lot of cleaning time. Remember Don Aslett's guide for telling the difference between important and unimportant things: "Don't love anything that can't love you back."

WHAT IS THE BIGGEST
HOUSECLEANING TIME-WASTER?

Picking up litter! Some homemakers are almost full-time "litter picker-uppers." This is not a progressive effort, because after you're through you're right where you should have been when you started. Solving the litter problem does more than free up your time: it's a great tension-reliever, because you're spared the constant worry, "If someone stops by now, what would they think of me?"

Another big liability of litter is that it causes time-consuming fights and frustration. When family members can't find their flung fatigues—even if they lost them themselves—everyone else has to take the blame as the seekers whine and stomp through the house trying to locate the article they should have put away in the first place. Litter/clutter causes more arguments than anything except finances.

A littered house is a worse visual and emotional offender than a dirty house because dirt has some natural authority, an excuse for being there. Dirt can be accepted to a degree: things get dirty with use, but litter is just personal possessions out of control.

Litter has three general causes:

1. Your family owns too much junk (excess toys, towels, trinkets, ties, playthings, furniture, books).
2. Your home has inadequate or inefficient storage spaces—racks, shelves, closets, hooks, towel bars, and toy boxes.
3. You have accepted the position of "family janitor" to a thoughtless bunch of litterers.

You are smart enough to cure all three; if you do, you'll cut the time you spend cleaning—and the hurtful anxieties of litter and clutter control—unbelievably.

MY FORMICA COUNTER TOP MARKS EVERY TIME I DRAG ANYTHING ACROSS IT.

"Formica" is a trade name for a plastic laminate used on walls, counters, furniture, etc. Several companies make different grades and qualities of countertop laminate, but Formica is tops in my book. Laminates have some outstanding characteristics, including durability, stain resistance, and *permanence*. Once glued down with contact cement they are there to stay. Damage or dissatisfaction with a color or other characteristic is not easy to change or fix—some colors and textures (a sad surprise to many people) are real losers to keep looking good, especially if they get heavy use. All laminates wear and lose their surface gradually making staining and marking tougher to remove.

Before you start the pitiful job of ripping Formica off, check your appliances' slide points—those small rubber or plastic tips fastened to the legs or bottom of the toaster, waffle iron, mixer, etc. Often they are the culprits leaving the marks. (If the problem is really bad, you can put on new points, but it's probably not worth it.) I use an Armorall-like product called Beauty Seal to revitalize my counters. Write to me at P.O. Box 39, Pocatello, ID 83204, for where to get Beauty Seal.

Choose your counter top wisely. Textured or matte surface laminates look rustic or homey, but mark worse and are tougher to clean than the smooth type. Patterns and fleched or marble designs camouflage marks nicely. Pure white is like wearing a white dress or suit and you know how that is! Remember, counter tops are something you clean every day, one of the most used areas in the home.

P.S. Because today's counter tops are ten times better than the linoleums of yesteryear, we often think we can use them as a chopping block, anvil, or hearthstone. Sharp kitchen tools and excessive heat will damage even the best product.

HOW DO YOU KEEP "DIRT PATHS" OUT OF YOUR CARPET?

I call these unsightly paths angling across your carpet "cow trails," because they look as bad as where a herd of cows, one following the other, walk across a plowed field. The good news (if it will make you feel any better) is that cow trails are on all carpets; they are the result of wear in the traffic patterns. The bad news is, because of the crushing and matting (and color change on some carpet), they show dramatically and everybody notices it.

The logical first step is to buy carpet in a color that camouflages the trails (gold, yellow, white, and pink are *not* cow trail-concealing colors). Any solid-color carpet will show traffic trails worse than a patterned one, and extremely light or dark colors are worse than mid-tones. (Medium earth-tone tweed is probably the best.) Sculptured or textured carpets also help hide cow trails.

The second step is to mat your entrances (see p. 104) to keep down the amount of dirt tracked into the house. Third (if your carpet is in and mats are installed) is to vacuum the traffic areas better and more frequently. Now here's a carpet-maintenance technique that will help keep those cow trails from ever getting dirty enough to require a major deep-cleaning. Assuming you have a good vacuuming program, most dirt accumulates on top of the carpet. To keep that surface dirt cleaned off, moisten a thick terry towel with carpet-cleaning solution, and run over the carpet. It will pick up and absorb surface grime and oils.

An inexpensive carpet rake will help rejuvenate mashed pile so it blends in with the rest of the rug. In some cases a plush nylon runner mat will be a dignified solution to the problem.

WHAT ABOUT THOSE PLASTIC COVERS TO PROTECT FURNITURE AND CARPET?

I presume you are referring to the clear plastic runners used over carpet and plastic slipcovers for upholstered furniture. I think they are the epitome of tackiness as well as real losers when it comes to maintenance and cleaning efficiency. If existing surfaces can't be used for what they were intended, why have them? Clear plastic carpet runners are visually offensive and present two different surfaces to be kept clean instead of one. Furniture arm covers (if used) are never on straight—if they're still on the arm at all. Slipcovers, too, often look "slipped" or wrinkled and are never of the same high quality as the furniture they cover. Why pay the price for a nice chair and cover it with a cheap-looking cover?

Plastic covers collect and *show* dust. Why deprive yourself of the pleasure of sinking down in a soft upholstered cushion—who wants to crackle down on a piece of cold plastic or tight-weave canvas cover? You bought the chair to enjoy, not exhibit. Think about that when you're planning your next purchase, and buy what you can comfortably make use of without having to cover. I highly recommend Scotchgard (a soil retardant) for upholstered furniture.

While on the subject, let me also address the "stick-em" shelf paper for cupboards. This "oilcloth" paper is trickier than you think to apply neatly and when you go to remove it, it leaves a sticky residue that collects lint and dirt, and makes for gobby painting.

Use good enamel paint or clear finish to line your shelves—and keep them clean! You'll find that this looks better—and in my opinion it's much more sanitary.

Q 38

WHEN IS THE BEST TIME TO DEEP CLEAN:

The best time to clean is a combination of when you feel like it and when things need cleaning, "House prouds" who clean by habit are wasting time and energy. These are the people who vacuum daily, dust hourly, right on schedule, sick or well, earth-quake or flood—whether it needs it or not.
You should clean:

WHEN—Dirt is producing a negative situation—appearance-, health-hazard-, or human-relations-wise—and before accumulating dirt and muck and grease begin depreci-ating your house.

WHEN—You are fresh and well. The great major-ity of successful, happy homemakers clean in the morning—that should tell you something.

WHEN—Every day for a few *minutes* instead of the once-a-week (or month) onslaught.

WHEN—The mess is fresh. The difficulty of clean-ing generally multiplies with procrastina-tion—not only will it take more work to clean it up "later"—but it'll be harder to gather the gumption to get started.

WHEN—You are scheduled to have minimum dis-tractions. Interruption is one of the big-gest deterrents to cleaning.

Contrary to popular belief, spring is possibly the *worst* time to do your heavy annual housecleaning. This longstanding ritual may have developed be-cause it took the beautiful spring weather to get up enough courage to face wax buildup, cobwebs, and twelve months of accumulated dirt in hard-to-get-at places. But spring is a time to get out and enjoy the fresh earth and air, flowers, and birds—not to be cooped up breathing ammonia fumes and sorting junk.

Fall, around the middle of October (or right after the Halloween window wax pranks, if your house is popular) is the best time to deep clean (for both you and your house). It's cool outside, the kids are in school and equipment and supplies are cheaper thanks to the fall sales. But more important, dust, damaging dirt, flies, bugs, tar, and other spots and debris that enter your home during the spring and summer months should be removed at the end of the summer. If it isn't, it stays around for the next eight months depreciating your house, increasing cleaning time and effort, and (believe it or not) draining you emotionally. Spring cleaning gives you a clean house for a month or two, like April and May, with the rest of the "heavy outdoors use" season, June through September, accumulating dirt and grime which remains in your house all winter. When you clean your house thoroughly in mid-fall, it will stay cleaner for a greater length of time—October, November, December, January, February, March, and April, and it's cleaner for the three major holidays: Thanksgiving, Christmas/Hanukkah, and New Year's. Fall is also a good time to paint inside and out. Try *fall cleaning* this year and see the difference it makes. Especially notice how much longer the windows stay clean—clean windows don't last long when a good spring rain and dust storm come along.

As for painting, try to select the driest time of year, when there's the least moisture in the air—which may or may not be fall, depending on where you live.

P.S. Use mats (see p. 104)—about 80% of what you clean up is tracked in by foot.

MY PET HAS HAD "ACCIDENTS" ON THE CARPET—HOW DO I GET THE ODOR OUT?

Odor control is not as simple as the TV aerial bombardment (aerosol perfuming) approach makes it sound—as I presume you've discovered. Ridding odors the TV way is generally masking them—or in plain talk, covering up the unpleasant odor with a stronger, more pleasant one. It's great while company is there, but later the old smell still penetrates your dwelling. There are also "odor neutralizers" available, which change the molecular structure of an odor so we won't smell it. They won't do anything for old pet stains, or new ones that have sunk into absorbent surfaces like carpet.

"Get rid of the odor source" means clean up whatever is causing the stink—pet piddle, dead mice, decayed food, or whatever. Shampoo the "accident" area with disinfectant cleaner solution, rinse, and dry. If the smell is just in the carpet pile, it will come out. But often "odors" in the form of liquid penetrate the carpet and get in the backing or pad, which is usually rubber, so it's difficult to get the smell out. (That's also why cars, couches, etc., that are exposed to tobacco or other smells for weeks are obnoxious for a long time.)

For truly effective odor control you must first remove the odor source, and then clean the carpet thoroughly. For this (and other nasty organic smells like vomit or sour milk) you need a *bacteria/enzyme digester* (available at pet stores) applied according to directions. (This product along with the whole realm of pet clean up is detailed in my book *Pet Clean-Up*

Made Easy, please write to me for where to get your copy.)

If your rug pad is permeated with odor, you might find it smart to replace it!

Air circulation and sunlight have a good neutralizing effect on odors, so don't underestimate the value of a fresh breeze here.

If you're a dog or cat lover and for one reason or another the prospect of endless vigilance against "accidents" looms before you, I'd advise that you use a soil retardant on your carpet *before* the problem occurs. Nylon carpets (and others made of man-made fibers) are less damageable (both by the original incident and by odor removal procedures).

P.S. A little time spent doing a proper job of house training your puppy initially beats a LOT of time (and bad temper) cleaning up "accidents" later.

I LOVE BLEACH TO CLEAN WITH, DO YOU?

Nope! Basically, bleach isn't a cleaner, it's a powerful oxidizer. It works great in the wash because its residue is always rinsed out. But just because things are *whitened* doesn't necessarily mean they're *clean*. Bleach's chemical power encourages its use as a rip-snorting, clean-all, kill-all, restore-all. But it actually isn't much of a cleaner, and is potentially very dangerous if used incorrectly.

Chlorine bleach, used regularly (even diluted), will deteriorate fabrics, chrome, plastic laminates (such as Formica) and many other surfaces. Bleach combined with any acid (such as bowl cleaner or vinegar) produces deadly chlorine gas, which has ended the career of more than one overeager bathroom cleaner. Add to this the danger of splashing or spilling it on skin, carpeting, clothing, or some other surface, and the injury or expensive damage this could cause. I'd recommend that you leave the bleach in the laundry room, and use it only as directed there.

YOU'VE SAID THAT MATS ARE THE MOST IMPORTANT TIME-SAVING INVESTMENT. WHY?

You should use mats *both inside and out* the entrances to your dwelling! At least 80% of the dirt in your home originates outside; and most of that comes in on people, stuck to their clothes and their feet. Where is your carpet the dirtiest? Right inside the door, on a $3' \times 4'$ area where a mat should be. Doesn't it make a lot more sense to shake out or vacuum a mat than to chase dirt all around the house?

FOR OUTSIDE—Use synthetic grass, or other rough surfaced mat with a rubber back to knock off the heavy residue from the feet, and avoid tracking in rain or snow. Heat or cold won't bother the mats much, and they are easy to maintain. I *wouldn't* advise you to mat the entire step or entrance area. Wall-to-wall exterior step carpet looks great, but it's expensive and once the used area "paths out" (wears out) the contrast between the worn and new-looking carpet will be ugly. Cover as much length of the main traffic area as you can.

FOR INSIDE—A good commercial nylon or olefin mat with a rubber or vinyl back is best all around for effectiveness, ease of cleaning, looks, lasting power, and safety (and it comes in great color choices)! These mats can be purchased at a janitorial supply store. Never use scatter rugs, throw rugs, or scabby remnants. Mats should be as wide as the door, generally three feet, and it should be at least four strides long.

Remember, the first principle of housecleaning is not to have to do it. Mats can clean more dirt out of your house just laying around than you can hustling around.

Q42

NOW THAT I'VE LEARNED HOW TO CLEAN LARGER WINDOWS WITH A SQUEEGEE*, WHAT DO I DO WITH MY JALOUSIES?

*(see *Is There Life After Housework?*, Chapter 7.)

I was asked this question by a Southern Belle with a heavy accent, and not having ever heard small panes called jalousies, I figured her husband was looking out the clean window at another woman and she was asking me to help cope with her jealousy. When five other women immediately joined in about their "jalousies," I asked them to explain. (Technically, jalousies are small louvered windows, but in the South the term refers to any small window, like the tiny multiple "Victorian" panes.)

Don't cut your squeegee down to midget size and try to use the squeegee method—it isn't worth it and you'll get a pain out of every pane. Bear in mind for starters that these small "checkered" windows are a big window area interrupted by numerous support sills, and that because of the distraction of the crisscrossing sills they don't show dirt, streaks, or specks like a big unbroken expanse of glass would. Small-pane windows were designed to give a house romantic appeal, so if spiders are holding hands in the corners, don't let it worry you, it just adds to the decor!

I'd use a plastic trigger spray bottle with a solution of alcohol-based window cleaner mixed up from concentrates, not glass 'waxes" or polishes. Spray the solution on and buff it dry with a soft clean absorbent cloth (paper towels won't hold up long enough for me). The fast-evaporating alcohol helps clean windows without leaving gunky buildup. If you do leave a streak, it probably won't be noticed on jalousies, as it would be on a big window. This solution will also wipe up the sills nicely after the windows are finished.

WHAT'S THE BEST WAY TO CLEAN OVENS?

Before you begin, don't believe anything comes "off easy." You've probably cleaned more ovens than I have, so you know that everything, including "miracle overnight soako's," end up to be hard dirty work. As a professional cleaner, I've seldom cleaned ovens, closets, refrigerators, drawers, or animals in houses, but in condominiums and apartments I've gotten my share. The only magic we found (using the type of oven cleaners that you do) was *patience*. Dope those sticky dudes down and don't be overanxious to get to the wiping off. Let the solution work even longer than it says on the label. It will almost surely save chiseling, scraping, and grinding. If it doesn't come clean in the first pass, don't scrub and fight it. *Recoat* it with oven cleaner until it does and save nine-tenths of the work. I like nylon scrubbing pads (such as Scotch-Brite)—they whip into the pesky spots around the elements, corners, and cracks.

Be sure the oven is off before you start! I'd advise you to wear rubber gloves to protect your dainty fingers from the harsh ingredients in oven cleaners, and remember that oven cleaners will damage tile, linoleum, and other surfaces if allowed to drip or splash and set for a while—be careful! (And protect your work area with an old sheet or cover.) Don't worry about stains on the racks, as long as the heavy buildups have been removed. Who looks into your oven anyway?

IF YOUR HOUSE NEEDS A COMPLETE CLEANING, WHERE SHOULD YOU START?

I'd start on the areas that go the fastest! Progress and glory are always encouraging (and besides you might get ammonia fatigue and someone else will have to finish what's left). Never start on a bathroom or kitchen—they always look the easiest but take the longest, and if cleaned first always get dirty in the process of cleaning other rooms. My crews were always slower when we started on kitchens, bathrooms, or trash-laden cubbyholes. Their dirt-killing instinct was dampened and their energy drained for the remaining work. Living rooms, halls, and family rooms are generally the fastest, most motivating areas to commence housecleaning, because they are generally less cluttered and furniture-filled and less dirty. They go fast, and because they seem to be a big part of the job, cleaners feel they are on the way to being done, so they really hustle on the remaining rooms.

As for order *within* a room, I'd clean ceilings, walls, and woodwork first, and windows, furniture, floors, and rugs last.

Ah . . . but before you start anything, I'd rustle some help (after draining the swimming pool, removing the TV tube, and hiding the golf clubs and car keys).

HOW DO I CLEAN BRICK?

This question, like many I get about inside masonry surfaces, is referring to bare or "raw" brick. Because the majority of brick surfaces are left untreated or unsealed they can easily be penetrated by stains and marred by abuse. Although masonry surfaces are low maintenance, you generally have a rough time getting them clean when they *do* need it. To begin with, because brick is so rugged-looking we aren't careful about dirtying it, and then its homely look prompts us to let it go longer than usual before trying to clean it. When we finally face the job, the brick has had years of attack from stains, fire, smoke, insect sprays, cellophane tape—you name it.

What to clean it with? Your friends have told you to use muriatic acid, because that's what professional bricklayers clean up with after a job. *Wrong*— muriatic acid isn't a cleaner; brickers use it to "wash" a brick surface after building it, because the acid dissolves the binders in the drops of mortar that may have spilled on brick during construction. Muriatic acid generally leaves a new brick surface looking sharp . . . but remember, mortar slop is all that was on it. *Your* brick is embellished with mustard, flyspecks, fireplace smoke, hand oils, dust, dustrag soil, glue, sand that has shifted loose, cooking oils, drink spills, etc.—muriatic acid won't help with most of those!

Step 1. Brush and vacuum the entire brick surface carefully to pull off/out every bit of sand or dust.

Step 2. Dry-sponge the entire area (see p. 24 re dry sponges).

Now you need to make a critical decision. Every

brick/stone masonry wall is different, in what it's made of and the resulting texture and hardness (e.g., sandstone is much softer and more porous than slate or travertine stone). If you have a hard non-porous surface to work with, you can use an ammonia solution and scrub brush. If you flood the wall and scrub like a demon, the dirt and crud will roll off in soapy waves. But if your brick/mortar is soft and porous, the solution might help drive the dinge permanently into the surface and you'll have a still-dirty wall with the wet look. That's why it's important to get as much of the loose dirt or film off as possible before you use any liquid that might "set" the dirt into the brick or mortar. If the brick wall is hard the dirt will float out—then you can absorb it with towels and scrub some more. When the cleaning water starts looking dirty, rinse with clear water and let it run off.

I've also cleaned many brick walls with just a dry sponge: both methods work well.

Fireplaces or brick walls that seem to be beyond help, can always be sandblasted. Sandblasting does a good job of cleaning but later you'll find sand in everything—Wheaties, salt shakers, shoes, clothes, makeup—*everything*. The easiest way to maintain masonry is to apply a coat or two of satin (low-sheen) masonry seal *before* a brick or stone wall gets dirty, or right after it's been cleaned/restored. Your wall will then present a surface that discourages dirt and is faster and easier to clean. Ask a reputable masonry dealer what low-sheen finish to use, and also ask about any special soft/porous stone or brick problem you are faced with. I always paint or stain my mortar joints after the wall is in place. It's easy to do and looks ten times as good as most drab concrete mortar—or attempts to mix color *into* the mortar.

On any brick or stone surface, whether you're planning to clean, paint, sandblast, or seal, try a small inconspicuous area first if you have any doubts.

WHAT IS A WET/DRY VACUUM?
DO I NEED ONE?

Do you *need* a dishwasher? The same is true of a wet/dry vacuum—if you have it, you'll use it to save your time and depreciation on the house. A wet/dry is exactly what its name implies: a vacuum that is capable of sucking up both wet and dry material. Wet/dry vacuums are an everyday commercial tool that have now joined the homemaker's arsenal. They are practical to own and easy to use in the home, and range in cost from $69.95 (for a local department store brand) to $450.00 (for a top-of-the-line commercial one). I'd recommend nothing larger than a ten-gallon capacity with a stainless or poly plastic tank. (Non-stainless metal tanks are okay but you have to keep them clean so they won't rust between uses.)

A wet/dry vacuum sucks up water or other liquid until the tank is full, at which point a float (which is like a rubber ball) will shut off the air pull (suction) and you'll know it's time to dump the tank, in the toilet or yard. Dry pickup uses a simple cloth filter.

You probably already know all the dry jobs you can use a vacuum for, but how about some of these *wet* jobs?

1. Picking up floor-scrubbing water (especially out of those cracks and pits in your floor).
2. Shampooing your own upholstery.
3. Cleaning up food and drink spills before they dry and stain.

4. Picking up vomit, potty spills, pet poop. (Don't gasp—this is a common and very real cleaning problem.) A wet/dry is a quick, sanitary way to do this. Then the surface can be rinsed and the water vacuumed away leaving things fresh and clean and odor-free.
5. Picking up sink, tub, and rain floods and over-flows inside and outside the house.
6. Emptying (from the top) plugged drains, sinks, toilets, goldfish bowls . . .

The most important wet/dry attachments to own are (1) a brush hand tool, (2) an upholstery tool, (3) a rubber-tipped squeegee floor tool. If you have some high dust-collecting areas—rough beams or whatever—you can get an extra extension hose. The directions that come with the machine will educate you in minutes to the basic maintenance needs of the unit.

A professional quality upright (Eureka is my favorite) and a commercial wet/dry with attachments is a great home vacuum combination that will last years if taken care of properly. That's about $500 for vacuums that will last you practically forever, and less than you pay for one "miracle super-duper vacuum."

WHAT IS THE FASTEST, EASIEST WAY TO CLEAN SCREENS?

HOW TO CLEAN SCREENS

Screens become imbedded with bugs, tree sap, dirt, bird droppings, other debris

FIRST if possible

TAKE SCREENS OFF before cleaning

Mix up a solution of heavy-duty cleaner or ammonia water

Lay the screens
flat on a soft
cloth, old rug,
or canvas pad

Scrub gently
with a soft
bristled brush

Rinse with hose

A sharp rap with
your hand will get
rid of excess
water

Let the sun
dry it

First: Always take them down—cleaning screens in place is ineffective and often damages them.

Second: Lay the screens on a flat, smooth, stable (cloth-covered) surface so cleaning and handling pressure won't stretch or bulge the face or pull the edge fasteners loose.

Third: Mix up some good strong heavy-duty cleaner or ammonia solution in a bucket and simply scrub the screens with a bristle brush.

Fourth: Rinse all the soap and loose dirt out with a hose, shake the worst of the water off, and re-install.

If your wet (rust-causing) climate and/or other conditions have gotten old screens to the point where they could use a paint job, you can buy screen paint and handy-dandy tools to paint or otherwise treat them after they are cleaned (screen paint is thin so it won't bridge—clog—the gaps). I don't generally like aerosols, but if you have only a few screens to do grab a can of spray paint—it's fast!

P.S. Any of you brittle-boned creatures over forty (like me)—remember that when you're taking down and putting up the screens you have both hands off the ladder, so be CAREFUL!

WHAT ABOUT BATHROOM CARPET?

It stinks! Don't put it in. If it's already installed, pray
. . . that your toilet never floods over. The chances
are 100% that a bathroom carpet will receive moisture regularly. When you step out of the tub or
shower you drip; the shower splashes over, around,
or under the curtain; and the boys have bad aim
when they are in a hurry or in the dark. Hair spray
settles in (and "super holds") it. And every toilet
floods over occasionally.

Carpet that gets wet regularly is stiff, fades, is
ugly and smells musty because it houses bacteria. It
rots. It is a haven for mildew, germ, and bug
growth. The next time you stay in a luxury hotel/
motel/condo with bathroom carpet, get down on
your knees and sniff—you won't want to walk on
it. Bathroom carpet takes more time to care for than
hard-surface flooring and will require more maintenance in the long run. It looks and feels great when
new, but it's only new for the first few days—then
it's downhill all the way.

If your bathroom carpet is presently in need of a
restorative cleaning job, be sure to use a disinfectant
cleaner in your shampooing solution, and extract all
the moisture you possibly can after rinsing.

HOW LONG DO OTHER WOMEN SPEND CLEANING?

For some strange reason, "How long (or how much time) do other people spend on cleaning?" is an important question. I suspect what they're really asking is: Am I doing more or less than my "share" of housework?

Ever since I began my professional housecleaning career in 1954 (at age 18) I've been asked this question, and ever since then I've been collecting information right from the source. For more than ten years now I've taught audiences of homemakers all over the U.S. and have asked them to fill out a comment card telling me how long they clean. I haven't compiled or computed all the feedback yet, but I analyzed a good geographical cross-section—several thousand cards from around the country—and found the following:

My informants made no distinctions, drew no lines—cooking, dishes, errands, home maintenance, floors, lawns, and the thousand other details that go into running a household all went under "housework." Aside from the discouraged who answer "How much time do you spend on housework?" with "25 hours" or "not enough," and the many who write, "too much," the calculations seemed to say that it took approximately 3.3 hours per day. (Remember this is an *average* that includes everything from single-person households to families of fourteen kids.)

Many moaned about their workload because of a big house. (I also collected information on the square footage of the average house and found that one-third of the people responding didn't know how big their houses were—a surprise to me as a builder.) Sheer house size is deceptive, because often a small, compact, densely furnished and decorated mobile home, for instance, will take more time to clean than a home three times its size. The age of a home influences how much time is spent, but the number and ages of the people using a home is the biggest factor determining time spent cleaning.

One of my discoveries (no surprise to the women) is the single biggest problem: 90% of the "mess" comes from husbands and children; 90% of the work is done by women! That's wrong!

Remember that you aren't racing anyone for honor. What *matters* is how happy you are, and the quality of your relationship with the other members of your household—not how many hours you spend cleaning or how fast you clean your house. Don't let the speed (or slowness) of other homemakers bother you—unless you are a born competitor, and then I suggest you clean your own house in a whip, start your own business (see Chapter 15 of *Is There Life After Housework?*), and capitalize on your accomplishments by becoming the fastest professional cleaner in the world.

IS IT CHEAPER AND BETTER TO MAKE YOUR OWN CLEANERS?

No! It's a joke! All those witches' brews and cleaning concoction recipes you find in books and magazines are desperate "fillers" of odd bits of space and that's about all they're good for. I'll bet there's not one in a hundred of those folks who merrily recommend that you use dried peach fuzz, ground bacon rind, dried bread crumbs, linseed oil, kerosene, a tea-spoon of vinegar or such who actually use them themselves. They all go to the supermarket or other supply source like everybody else and buy cleaners that are cheaper, better, safer, and easier to use.

It's not your moral, money-saving duty to mix your own brew (it's not even paternal or maternal, nor is it patriotic). Most people don't dig their own worms for fishing any more, so why should you feel obliged to pioneer beeswax and barley into home-made furniture polish? I guess it's a carryover of the American tradition—we feel we're being disloyal to our "home duties" if we don't make *some* of our own domestic needs—clothes, cleaners, canned fruits, etc.

Prepared chemicals, polishes, waxes, and supplies are safer, more convenient, and much cheaper in the long run. Making your own cleaners requires gathering (often expensive) ingredients and addi-tives, and then containers to mix and store them in. You take not only your time but a big risk by com-bining chemicals that might be physically harmful.

It isn't worth it. Buy concentrated cleaners from a janitorial supply house and mix with water in a spray bottle—that will satisfy any yearnings for hav-ing a hand in making your own "home brew."

IF YOU HAD TO CHOOSE BETWEEN WALLPAPER, WALLCOVERING, AND PAINT, WHICH WOULD YOU PICK?

Two to one I would paint; however, I might be prejudiced because I'm a professional painter and find application and maintenance of paint pretty simple.

I would eliminate wallpaper entirely and stick to vinyl wallcovering. *Installation* is the biggest cost when you cover a wall, so why put on paper that will mark, tear, and stain easily, yet be difficult to clean?

If I were an expert paperhanger, and knew all the ins and outs of handling weaves, foils, and flocks, I'd probably like wallcovering as much as I do paint.

When I *do* use wallcoverings, I use easily maintainable, smooth-surface material. Damage is sure to come to every wall in the form of stains, scuffs and gouges, etc.—select a wallcovering that will clean and be repaired easily.

The condition of your walls and your decorating taste are the real factors in the choice. Scabby, cracked, uneven walls, even with a good paint job, still look cheap and unattractive, plus it generally takes double the effort to paint such a wall.

Wallcovering can make a room brighter, warmer, more inviting, even more luxurious. It can also help establish its character. Good-quality vinyl wallcovering can also serve a practical function as a wall finish. A patterned wallcovering instantly hides defects and upgrades the appearance not only of the wall, but the space. With their vinyl surfaces and tough fabric backings, wallcoverings put a good cleanable finish over many surfaces ranging from new sheet rock to old plaster. On wallboard, sheet rock, and plywood, they minimize joints, cracks, and nail pops. On plaster, they can bridge rough spots and cracks and add structural reinforcement. They also offer long-term performance. They're durable, resistant to fading and abrasion, and easy to maintain.

While the initial investment for wallcovering is greater, its life is generally more than double that of paint. You usually have to repaint every three years or so, while the normal life of vinyl wallcovering is nine to ten years, depending on how you use the house.

Wallcovering comes in different grades, and I can only advise, "It costs a dollar less to go first class." High-quality covering can usually be more easily installed, lasts longer, and of course—the important part—is easier to clean.

If you choose to paint, use a low-gloss satin enamel paint in a nice off-white, accent a few walls with dark colors, then let furniture, drapes, and decorations carry the burden of making the room feel good. In painting as in wallcoverings, go for the best! The more expensive paint will eventually save you time and money.

Q52

IS THERE ANY SUCH THING AS A "CLEAN" COLOR?

White, of course, is psychologically clean. It's become synonymous with purity and hence we accept—"the whiter, the cleaner." Even though white uniforms, walls, furniture, rugs, and vehicles get dirtier faster, because white doesn't hide or disguise dirt or soil, people trust it. Whites (off-whites) look great in house interiors (walls are one of the most noticeable parts of a home), and can be easily touched up or patched if nail holes or gouges need repairing. Many a handsome home uses off-whites for walls and woodwork and lets drapes, carpet, and furniture (rather than colored walls) add the color.

Yellow is a tough color to "cover" when painting walls, and the hardest to make look good when you're cleaning upholstery or rugs. Yellow broadcasts any darker color against it (that's why so many signs and book covers use yellow backgrounds)—and this includes marks or dirt. It's a cheerful color, but when interrupted (which dirt and marks tend to do) you unconsciously dislike it. Yellow and gold carpet are the toughest of all to keep looking good after use, even after cleaning. Blue is another color that's difficult to keep looking good, probably because blues are quiet and restful, so dirt and marks seem more of an intrusion.

Browns and beiges are thought of as earthy or natural colors and hence, dirt and cobwebs, nicks, marks, and handprints won't grate on your nerves as much as they would on light golds or blues. In general, pastels and light shades of any color are hard to maintain, as are extremely dark colors (these even show light dust!). Solid colors show more dirt than patterns and textures. If you're *really* interested in hiding dirt, use mid-range tweeds with deep textures on everything you can.

IS THERE A SMART APPROACH TO BED-MAKING?

Yes! Minimize the number of blankets and covers you use—a couple of thick ones are better than four thin ones that you'll be half the morning smoothing and straightening out. Buy or make a comforter quilt that serves as a bedspread too, with decorative trim that follows the bed contours. (Be sure the comforter has a cover that zips off for easy laundering.) Don't have excess or overly decorated pillows or dust ruffles for "fanciness"—they end up being a pain in the neck!

If there are several different sizes of beds in the house (king, queen, double, twin, hide-a-bed), have different-colored linens for each one to save struggling with the wrong sheets on the wrong bed.

Learn how to make a bed so that you only walk around it once; the hotel professionals do it that way (that means don't spread one cover, then circle, tuck, spread, circle, tuck, etc.). Spread all the covers from one side, then circle around, tucking as you go. Make friends with a housekeeper from a large hotel nearby and have him or her teach you.

WHAT DO I DO ABOUT MY GARAGE? (after my massive garage sale)

It doesn't cost much (in fact *less*) to be clean. For example—three 8-foot 2×12's and a few cinderblocks can offer order, safety, and convenience in the form of instant garage storage shelves. Go into your garage and look around. Here are a few "rules" (ideas) that will help you:

1. Store anything light by hanging it as high as reachably possible. This keeps it out of the "stumbling over" path, yet readily accessible.
2. Find, buy, or make a wall cabinet (six feet tall if possible) to store small hand tools, paint and lawn chemicals, etc. Concealing stuff that must be stored in the garage provides emotional as well as physical advantages.
3. If you wish to mount or hang frequently used hand tools (or display them for friends), the smart, practical, and economical way is to install a $4' \times 8'$ piece of quarter-inch pegboard on the wall (just like you see in store displays)— you can do it easily and a variety of peg hardware is available.
4. Make sure you can see! Most garages are inadequately lighted, which makes them feel like a mine shaft instead of part of a home. The wiring is usually adequate; just convert the incandescent fixtures into fluorescent tube lights. It will make the garage look better and be safer and cheaper.
5. Paint the garage walls—90% of garages are un-

finished, and thus look naked and shabby. Two coats of a good enamel (new or left over from another job) can be applied for pennies and reward you for years. If the walls are bare studs, put up sheet rock and then paint it.

6. Prepare and seal the floor, if it's concrete. This will make it fast and easy to maintain and improve the looks and feel of the garage.

To seal your garage floor, remove all possible furniture, tools, etc., from the floor; sweep up all the surface dirt. Mop on a solution of strong alkaline cleaner, or better yet, etching acid diluted in water. (Your janitorial supply house or paint store has these—with specific directions on the label.) Let it soak in awhile; if the floor is old and marked, you can scrub it with a floor machine. Flush the solution off—preferably using a floor squeegee—and rinse with a hose. Allow the floor to get good and dry, then apply transparent concrete seal or an all-purpose seal, either of which can be obtained at a paint or janitorial supply store. Apply the seal—according to directions—with any applicator that will distribute it in a nice thin even coat, and let it dry. I'd advise a second coat to ensure that all the rough surfaces are filled.

There's no reason to have a garage that embarrasses you. With a little planning and work, it can look like the part of your *home* that it is.

HOW OFTEN SHOULD YOU CLEAN DRAPES?

Why am I asked this question so often? It's like asking, "How often should I take a bath?" It all depends on:

1. The kind of drapes you have (fiberglass, lined, sheer, pleated, etc.). Nylon, for instance, doesn't get dirty as quickly as cotton, and textured drapes don't show dirt.
2. Where they are (heavy-use area, a study, food area, etc.).
3. The amount of use and abuse they get (number of kids/cats climbing on them).
4. The professional cleaning facilities available (and their cost).
5. How the drapes look now.
6. How difficult they are to re-hang (and who has to hang them).

The average drape-cleaning span in a home is every other year, depending on how dusty your neighborhood is and the heating/ventilating system you have. If they're old, inexpensive drapes, I'd let them go past tolerable, then replace them. If the abuse level (sun, moisture, kids, animals) is high and drapes are of good quality, I'd probably clean them every year. Make a visual check and when they're soiled and stained, clean them. Remember, however, that one of the drawbacks of drapes is that they always fade—and fading won't be fixed by cleaning.

When you select your window coverings, remember the window area is a target for activity. The light draws bugs, kids, pets, and people and the convection currents here draw airborne soil. Tinted or smoked glass, vertical blinds, decorative screens and other alternative window coverings might be worth considering. When you buy and install drapes and curtains, go simple—choose styles and materials that are easy and economical to maintain.

WHAT IS THE CLEANEST HEAT?

The SUN! You can't beat it. After the sun, you might imagine a great difference between electric, gas, hot water, oil, wood, and coal heat—there isn't. "Dirty" coal furnaces were blamed for many a grossly dirty house for many a year. But the dirt really wasn't from the coal (or residue from the coal)—that went up the chimney. More coal dust came in through the door than through the vents. Only warm air from your furnace ambles out of the vents—and clean air doesn't dirty things. Radiant or convection or "still" heat is a bit cleaner than forced-air heat (whether oil, electric, or gas)—the movement of the circulating air can push around the dirt already present in a house or room. And of course, we all know that good clean furnace filters make a real difference.

The prime reason for dirty homes in the old coal- and wood-burning days was poor insulation and weatherstripping. Homeowners who put clean electric heat in an old home without reinsulating found to their surprise that their walls got almost as dirty as in the coal days. And those now burning wood (or coal) in newer, well-insulated houses don't have dirty walls. Because of the temperature differential, poorly insulated outside walls pull filth to the inside walls. The wood itself in wood heating systems can create the need for clean up, as can leaky seams in woodstove pipe.

I'd advise you to insulate well and select the heat that's most economically sound for your area and lifestyle—you'll notice little if any difference in the dirt level. Before you blame greasy walls or inside window films on your oil, coal, or gas furnace, check your *cooking venting system*—the problem is probably more the hamburger than the heat source.

WHAT DO YOU THINK OF "LEMON OIL" POLISHES/ CLEANERS FOR WOOD?

First off . . . "lemon oil" is not a cleaner! And it may surprise you to know that it usually has nothing to do with lemons. Lemon oil is made from a high-grade paraffin oil, then lemon scent is added for "fragrance." The same is true of the aerosol lemon-scented silicone wood polishes (the TV wonders!)—the lemon smell is just to sell you.

Properly used, lemon oil can be of some help in maintaining wood. Lemon oil is a penetrant like most oil; it will soak in, condition, and even harden bare wood. This not only helps keep the wood from drying out, but helps protect it from dampness, stains, etc. Lemon oil doesn't really have much value on coated (varnished, painted, shellacked) wood surfaces because it can't pass or be absorbed through the membrane coating and tends to dry slowly and remain tacky, catching dust. Old furniture, even if it appears shiny, often has invisible cracks that allow the oil to seep in and help condition the wood. If lemon oil (or any oil) is overused it will build up just like the aerosol gunk spray polishes (top woodworkers basically say polishes should be removed each time before applying more).

There is a big fascination for natural unfinished wood today—if you have such a finish that must be "fed," lemon oil is good for the purpose (as long as the wood in question isn't in *culinary* use, in which case you must use mineral oil, or vegetable oil). Personally I wouldn't have furniture that requires constant oiling and feeding or constant polishing. Feeding a family takes enough time and money.

If your wood cleaners haven't cleaned the wood kitchen cabinets, it isn't your fault. Lemon oil isn't a cleaner! (Instead, use a grease-dissolving detergent solution.)

HOW DO YOU CLEAN
HOUSEHOLD GARBAGE CANS?

About once a month or so—after emptying the cans—I take my trusty bathroom spray bottle, squirt a heavy mist of disinfectant cleaner solution on them (inside and out), let them sit for awhile, then wipe them out and rinse them. If tenacious deposits persist, use your trusty nylon toilet brush. In a hurry I've even turned my containers over a sprinkler head—that spray gets them pretty clean.

How often a pail should be cleaned depends on the size of your household and the area it is used in. For example, a sewing room wastebasket goes months; a bathroom container—that has to contend with used dental floss, smeary makeup remover wipes, etc.—needs more frequent cleaning. And the kitchen can—filled with dripping cartons, apple cores, and uneaten scrambled eggs—needs routine attention!

I'm not wild about garbage can "liners" (except for the kitchen) because they're expensive, unsightly, take up storage space and burden the environment. But liners *do* make can-cleaning easier, if you like using them well enough to pay for them.

WHAT ARE THE BEST CLOTHES TO WEAR WHEN CLEANING?

That's a good question—clothes do make a difference. (You should have seen the janitor fashion show at our last cleaning convention! My wife refused to model the dual toilet plunger bra.)

COLORS. Whites are good for one reason: your accomplishment is magnified because paint or dirt shows and looks like progress. That's why professional painters and cleaners wear "whites."

SHOES. Tennis shoes or rubber-bottomed shoes are great for climbing around, traction on ladders, etc. Shocks from plugs, appliances, or fixtures are also less likely with rubber or vinyl shoes. High heels are *out*, too, and never attach cleaning tools to your feet!

HANDS. If you have allergies or sensitive skin (or are working with strong cleanser or corrosive materials) use rubber gloves. But otherwise it isn't worth having sweaty robot fingers.

Loose, unbinding, *thick* clothes are best! But don't wear clothes that hang down or bag so much that they catch on ladders or corners or other projections. Wear long pants, jeans, or coveralls, not shorts—bare arms are okay; bare legs get pinched on ladders, or while kneeling. Long sleeves and shirts left out, not tucked in, keep dirt and falling debris off your body. Wear something you're not afraid to ruin. Don't dress up; people who claim they feel so much better about cleaning while dressed up never get much done. It takes a lot of psychic energy to get dressed to the hilt. Remember: you are *cleaning* (working), not putting yourself on display. You are there to have your *results* admired, not you, so dress accordingly. Remove jewelry, and tie your hair up if it's long and will get in the way. If your glasses fall off easily, hold them on with an elastic fastener around the back.

P.S. Don't go out of your way to dress like a slob. Feeling *negative* about yourself isn't going to make the job any easier.

WHY CAN'T I GET MY SPONGE MOP CLEAN?

Because too many people have been convinced that water is all that's needed to clean the modern floor. Well, dirt is not modern, it's the same old thing and needs a cleaner to dissolve and release dirt from whatever it's clinging to (in this case, the floor and the mop). Use a little all-purpose neutral cleaner in your cleaning water, and you'll have a cleaner floor and mop.

Dirt has a tendency to stick to surfaces, especially a cloth or sponge. Unless there's some soap or detergent there to cause the dirt to release so it can be rinsed out, your tool will remain soiled. Using a good cleaner will not only work miracles on your floor it'll help keep your mop clean. When your mop stays dirty it's a good indication that your floor or other surface is also dirty.

Many people try to "bleach" their mops clean. This isn't very smart—bleach is a harsh oxidizer and will reduce the life of the tool. No sponge mop will look brand new after being used, so don't worry about a slight discoloration.

WHAT DO I DO ABOUT HARD WATER SPOTS ON MY WINDOWS?

First, eliminate the culprit (sprinkler, hose, etc.) that's causing the problem. Don't blame it on rain—rainwater is soft and doesn't leave mineral deposits.

Use a mild phosphoric acid cleaner to dissolve mineral deposits on outside glass. Most janitorial supply houses will have one or more products of this type under various trade names and weaker solutions are available in supermarkets as such products as LimeAway. A non-abrasive white nylon scrub pad can be used to speed the work. After removing the deposits, clean the window with your squeegee. Long-standing hard water deposits may have fused with the surface and be unremoveable.

Don't use colored scrub pads, steel wool, or sponges, as they have abrasives in them that can scratch glass. Also, don't use strong acid cleaners such as toilet bowl cleaners or drain cleaners. They can damage metal, brick, paint, and hands.

Mild acid cleaners are also safe to use for deliming bathroom sinks, chrome fixtures, and tub and shower units.

HOW DO YOU CLEAN CARPETED STAIRS AND CARPET EDGES?

The bad news is that carpet edges—the one or two inches next to the baseboard or stairs that the vacuum never seems to get—are one of the most telltale signs of poor housekeeping. A trained eye will pick it up two seconds through your front door. The good news is that those dusty edges don't hurt a thing except your ego. Because edges are not exposed to traffic (which means no physical damage to the carpet) the problem is mostly visual. I'd recommend you vacuum the edge with your vacuum attachments, not more than once a year. The rest of the time, sweep any visible cobwebs, dirt, or dust away from the base- or mopboards with a broom or damp towel, then do your regular vacuuming.

Stairs, though a little trickier than regular carpet edges, I'd treat the same way. The back and side edges of stair carpets receive little or no traffic so dirt doesn't damage them. The step—especially the center two feet—gets 90% of the abuse, and it is heavy! Once a month or so, get someone to hold the vacuum and quickly take a small nozzle (to concentrate suction) and vacuum the edge. Or you can take a damp towel, get on your hands and knees, and in about five minutes whip down the stairs removing the fur/dust from the edges. For the center of the stair, use your beater upright or canister vacuum. If it's too heavy to use on the stairs once a week, I'd say it's too heavy to use anywhere in the house. You can purchase a nice commercial Eureka upright vacuum that will do a super job on all routine household vacuuming.

THE "JOINTS" (GROUT) IN MY BATHROOM TILE ARE GRUNGY— HOW DO I CLEAN THEM?

The typical grungy shower has a buildup of body oils and soap scum as well as hard water deposits, maybe mildew too. I'd clean it first with a good degreaser solution, this will cut the oils. Then hit it with a mild phosphoric acid (the base of many tile- and grout-cleaning compounds); the best I've used is Showers N Stuff. It's less dangerous to use than harsh acids and does just as well. As a last resort a 1:5 chlorine bleach/water solution is helpful in killing mildew and whitening stained grout, and it won't damage ceramic tile.

Dirty mortar joints are a universal problem that can be reduced, if not prevented, by some precautionary measures:

1. Always make sure grout is sealed before you use it. Your masonry or tile dealer can tell you what you will need, and show you how to do it. Grout is best sealed when new. Once oils, stains, and moisture have penetrated it, sealing is less effective.
2. Squeegee or wipe down the shower walls after every use.
3. Clean regularly with a disinfectant cleaner, and in the long run you'll spend less time "grout routing."
4. If you're building or remodeling, use darker mortar. It looks nice and eventually will help hide the problem.

Avoid miracle tub and shower mortar whiteners— most of them are just more expensive versions of the household bleach solution. And remember that bleach is just an oxidizer, so its results are just temporary.

Q 64

WHAT'S THE ONE SINGLE THING I CAN DO TO BECOME THE PERFECT HOUSECLEANER MY HUSBAND HARPS ABOUT?

Pick one of your toughest housecleaning/housework weeks. Leave town, fake sick, volunteer for a week of jury duty (or die, if necessary), and have your husband assume your role and the duties and rewards that go with it. Or let your mother-in-law have control—she'll beat your "BABY" into shape and he'll never again say, "Well, Mother used to . . ." You'll be perfect by the end of the week.

WHY DO MY FLOORS GO DARK UNDER MATS AND APPLIANCES?

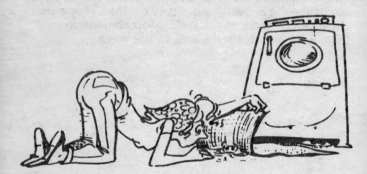

It could be old wax yellowing, but it could also be the flooring material itself. Most floor coverings and paints will yellow if kept in the dark for an extended period of time. The ultraviolet rays in normal sunlight (or even artificial light) have a bleaching action and tend to keep white materials white. When kept in the dark, away from this natural whitening action, most flooring materials—even enamel paint—tend to darken and yellow with age. If you've ever removed a picture from a painted wall and found a permanently darkened area behind it, you know what I'm talking about.

There is no easy cure for this phenomenon, as this type of yellowing has become a part of the paint or flooring itself and cannot be cleaned off.

Many people don't use floor mats for this reason. Personally, I *like* the yellowing under mats—it forces you to keep the mats in place, resulting in a longer-lasting floor and a cleaner house. The benefit of matting to you, your floors, and the entire house (see p. 104) far outweighs the risk of slight discoloration "where a mat was!"

HOW DO YOU CLEAN A
TELEPHONE?

The doorknob is the dirtiest thing in a house, but the telephone has to be running a strong second in the filth finals! An assortment of dirty (and often oily) ears, hands, mouths, and cheeks are in close germ-spreading communication with a phone every day—so use a disinfectant cleaner solution in a plastic spray bottle when you clean the phone, which should be often. A phone in a home should be cleaned at least monthly, and weekly—not weakly—in a commercial building.

Never spray a phone directly, especially in the area of the transmitter holes on the handpiece because moisture might cause a malfunction. Spray the solution onto a soft clean cloth and wipe the phone, then polish with a dry cloth.

HOW DO I CLEAN MY "COTTAGE CHEESE" CEILING?

The sprayed-on "cottage cheese" type ceilings have a rough look but this is actually a soft pliable finish, generally made of little coated beads of styrofoam, which act not only as a beautifying "texture," but also as an acoustical surface. The combination of its rough texture and its soft, absorbent properties make a cottage cheese ceiling very difficult to clean even with the dandy dry sponge. When cleaning is necessary, if a dry sponge or a vacuum dust brush won't do it (and the ceiling soil is only normal), the oxidizing treatment outlined on pages 24–25 will do a good job of making it appear cleaner.

You have one last alternative: spraying or rolling on a coat of paint (a real job). I would use a latex flat finish paint and a deep-pile roller, if you roll. Painting this surface restores the fresh, clean look of a new ceiling, but it might retard the acoustical value.

The liabilities of this type of ceiling finish far outweigh the assets.

If you have the cottage-cheese-with-glitter version, my heart goes out to you. There is simply no effective way to clean this kind of ceiling. Once it starts looking bad, about the only sensible recourse is to paint it.

Next time, tell your architect you want a ceiling texture that is attractive and *cleanable*.

IS ALUMINUM ALWAYS
SO UGLY . . . ?

Be satisfied with aluminum: it doesn't rust, fade, scale, scab, chip, or rot. It might oxidize a little (that cloudy gray film on the surface) but it still looks okay without much maintenance. Most aluminum, whether on inside or outside fixtures (especially window structures), has a burnished or brushed—not shiny and smooth surface—and is not intended to look spit-polished all the time.

But if the oxidation gets intolerable to you, mix up any good cleaning solution, rub it on, and wipe it dry. This won't change the aluminum's appearance much, but there'll be a lot of black marks on your rag, psychologically creating the impression that the aluminum is now clean—and you'll live happily ever after.

WHERE DO YOU DRAW THE LINE BETWEEN CLEAN ENOUGH AND TOO CLEAN?

As my Grandma (a mother of fifteen children who always had a clean house) said, "If the dishes are on the sink ready to do and my husband wants me at that moment to be or go someplace with him (fun or work), that's clean enough!" Or as a woman in Randolph, Utah, wrote on a seminar comment card, "I can tolerate dust till it's ankle-deep, I'd rather rock babies 'cause babies don't keep."

Somewhere between the health hazard, Bertha Buried, and the compulsive cleaner, Annie Septic, is a standard that fits your values, energies, available time, and personal need for cleanliness and order. Decide on the level of cleanliness, order, and sanitation that suits you emotionally, physically, and financially, and hold to it; remember that *you* must be comfortable with the level—double standards never work. That means when Mae Tickulus comes to your house, you can't quickly immaculatize the dwelling, then tolerate an inch of sawdust on the floors the next week when the Cub Scouts are carving totem poles in your basement.

There is "clean" dirt and "dirty" dirt. There's no sin in *making* a mess—all accomplishment requires a mess of some kind—the sin is in *leaving* the mess. Thousands of chronic cleaners have swept family and friends out the door because they didn't know when clean was clean enough. And an equal number of "grime lovers" have accomplished the same thing with slop and disorganization.

We clean for 3 basic goals:
1. Beauty (it looks and feels good)
2. Health (germ killing)
3. Economy (clean cuts depreciation)

Q70

I HAVE DEEP-TEXTURED WALLCOVERING AND I'M READY TO GIVE UP TRYING TO CLEAN IT.

You remove dirt and film from any indented or textured surface in two stages:
(1) dissolve
(2) wipe/remove
Too many of us are used to wiping off easy smooth enamel surfaces and forget that *dissolving and suspending* is the number one approach to any cleaning. Mere wiping just glides over the little pockets full of dirt. If you use the right cleaning solution, the deposit in the grooves will soften and "float" loose so that a thick terry cloth or a mild brushing action will extract it. Apply a warm solution of all-purpose cleaner to the wallcovering; a lather can be worked up on the vinyl using a soft-bristled brush. Rinse thoroughly with clean water, changing the water frequently. Give extra attention to removing suds or soap and loosened dirt from the depressed areas of deeply embossed wallcovering; drying the surface well with a terry towel should absorb any cleaning residue.

Remember, wallcoverings generally contain a chemical compound called a "plasticizer." The plasticizer is necessary to condition and soften the vinyl so it can be rolled and applied easily. If dirt is allowed to stay on the surface for a long time, the plasticizer tends to absorb dirt, making the wallcovering even more difficult to clean.

Many stubborn surface stains can be removed with isopropyl alcohol on a hanky-size cloth. (Do not use carbon tetrachloride or lacquer solvents for cleaning vinyl wallcoverings.)

DOES SCOTCHGARD PAY?

It does for the 3M Company! "Scotchgard" is a trade name for a soil retardant used on carpet/rugs or upholstery. 3M also has a soil retardant specifically for carpeting called "Carpet Protector." Several companies besides 3M make soil retardants.

Guarding against penetration of soils, liquids, and stains by applying a protective coating generally does pay: Scotchgard does an excellent job on 95% of the upholstery fabric I've used it on or seen it used on. It preserves and protects, makes the units look better and wear longer. On carpet I'll make that about 75%, because people have a tendency to let treated surfaces go, even though dirt still gets on them.

Scotchgard (or other soil retardants) will pay if:

1. Carpet or upholstery are prepared by thorough cleaning prior to application.
2. It is applied right. (Follow the *directions*.)
3. The surfaces are maintained thereafter. Too many people think soil retardant-treated surfaces are self-maintaining—they don't have to be cleaned ever again. This mental sanctification often makes the retardant do more harm than good because we stop taking care of that surface at all.
4. The fabric's manufacturer okays soil retardant use.

And last. . . .

5. If you hire a professional to do it, get references.

Q72

I GET LEAKS AND YELLOW STAINS ON MY OUTSIDE WALLS IN LATE WINTER AND EARLY SPRING, EVEN THOUGH MY ROOF IS IN PERFECT SHAPE.

The thawing and freezing of early spring cause an ice buildup on the eaves/gutter area of the roof. This buildup often acts like a dam, trapping melt-and-runoff water, and causing it to back up *under* the shingles or tile roofing. The water leaks through and causes the wood of the roof to swell and rot. It will deteriorate/stain the wall material itself (paneling, sheet rock, plaster) and also hurt the paint or wall-covering, causing more cleaning for you.

Take care to keep ice off the eaves. It can be chipped off with a hand tool, but the best way is to heat cable the buildup area (usually the north side). Heat cable (sometimes called "heat tape") is a simple electrical wire that looks like a heavy extension cord. It warms up when it's plugged in, and when it's laid in the gutter or buildup areas of the roof it keeps ice from accumulating.

Real moisture stains on exterior or interior walls (those awful yellow-brown splotches) are from saturated, dissolving sheet rock and generally can't be removed. A quick paint touchup is the answer, but it's wise to undercoat or use a sealer or shellac on the stain first so it won't bleed through.

WHERE CAN I GET PROFESSIONAL CLEANING SUPPLIES AND EQUIPMENT?

The quality, time-savings, and safety of professional supplies make it worth the effort to seek them out; they're cheaper in the long run, too, although they may *seem* more expensive because they're often in concentrated form. Most people live within range of a reputable janitorial supply house (look in the Yellow Pages right now); big cities should have several.

When you go into these stores, feel welcome and don't act like a cow in a circus. Act like the professional you are! (You've scrubbed more sinks than a lot of professional janitors anyway.) The staff will help you choose the best tools for the job at hand and give you expert instruction on how to use them, as well as professional chemicals in the amount you will need. What they don't stock, they can get for you. Most of them buy from a distributor/jobber or direct from a factory outlet at a 40-50% discount, and on a cash deal most of them will turn around and give you 20-30% discount off retail, especially if you gang together a few of your neighbors for buying power! If you live in a small town like me (McCammon, Idaho—population 720), save up until you get to the big town, then splurge (you should only have to visit the store once a year anyway)!

Watch the papers under *Miscellaneous For Sale*, or watch for bankruptcy or business closeouts—used professional cleaning equipment is tough to get rid of, so you'll get some good deals. I saw a friend pick up a (dirty but in perfect shape) 13-inch Holt buffer ($299) for $5. I picked up a $600 Clarke floor machine and a big $1,200 extractor—$250 for both. Look for the 12-13 inch commercial floor machines for bonneting your carpet, look for a good upright or wet/dry vacuum (preferably the five-gallon size), even mop buckets. The Equipment Chart at the back of the book lists the professional supplies and equipment most likely to be useful to a homeowner. Buy your chemical cleaners in concentrated form and dilute them yourself. The quality of professional materials will save you tons of money and time.

To order professional tools and supplies by mail, send a postcard with your name and address for a free catalog/newsletter to:

Clean Report
P.O. Box 39
Pocatello, ID 83204

Q74

MY WHITE METAL CUPBOARDS ARE CLEAN, BUT DULL-LOOKING. WHAT CAN I DO?

Many homes have cupboards which were originally painted with white or other colors of enamel. Because of aging (mostly caused by cleaning) they don't have their original "gloss depth." If a surface is dulled—even a glass surface—it has little reflective value and hence no shine. As enamel cupboards (metal or wood) grow dull, they become tougher to clean and never look as classy, even if the original coat of paint is still intact. Constant use of powdered cleansers and scouring pads depreciates them faster than using soft white nylon pads and neutral cleaner solution. Ultraviolet light (sunlight) in time will gradually yellow them. It's purely an aesthetic problem but if lack of shine or a yellowish color bothers you:

1. Aways polish with a dry towel after cleaning to remove any scum.
2. After they are clean, use a light coat of transparent silicone finish (such as Armorall). This takes a little time to apply every so often but it will restore the reflection.
3. Replace them—but I wouldn't. Most metal cupboards are strong and straight, and new cabinets (including removal of old and hanging new) can cost $4,000-$10,000. Besides, you'll end up with a pile of old cupboards that you'll never throw away "because they're still in perfect shape" (except for the shine).
4. Have them repainted—don't faint. There is a

process called electrostatic painting: we paint appliances, office desks, files, bookcases—anything metal with it. It's non-messy, and looks and wears much better than conventional hand or spray methods. It's the neatest thing you've ever seen.

Electrostatic painting uses a basic law of electricity: opposites attract. Here's how it works:

The article to be painted is given a negative charge. The paint is given a positive charge and atomized through a special revolving nozzle. The object attracts the paint droplets just as a magnet attracts iron filings, and instead of being sprayed on, the paint is actually *plated* on!

The electrostatic force is so powerful it can actually pull paint around corners. It wraps paint around the object to give a smooth, even coat. Most important, there's no overspray, no fogging or drift, no blast-through as with conventional spray guns. It is amazingly neat and clean.

Often, if you just want to do the fronts of your cupboards, you can do the job without emptying your shelves. And if your cupboards have been previously painted, a light sanding will prepare them for the bonding of the electrostatic process.

If you are tired of white, there is a great color choice. Look in the Yellow Pages or ask around and you'll locate some companies that do electrostatic painting.

HOW DO YOU CLEAN OFF MASKING TAPE AND OTHER STICKY RESIDUE?

First, you pull off what will come off (remember, when it's fresh it *all* comes off). If it's been on awhile, which is what I presume you're referring to—such as when you tape around a window to stop air leaks or use masking tape to hang a poster— when you try to get it off you'll leave some of the glue and parts of the tape. Acetone or nail polish remover will soften and loosen the glue base so the tape residue can be removed. These removers won't harm glass, baked enamel (such as on refrigerators), or other non-reactive surfaces, but can harm some paint and plastic surfaces. Be sure to test in an inconspicuous place before you use it on a surface you're not sure of. De-Solv-it is a popular citrus-based remover. Lacquer thinner takes mastic off easily—be careful what you use it on.

Don't use masking tape any more than you need to. For painting, a good slant-tip sash brush in most people's hands can cut a finer line than with the tape's help!

P.S. To hang posters, drive tiny nails—they never fail and leave only a minute hole when removed.

HOW ABOUT USING KEROSENE AS A CLEANER?

It's outdated!

The reason some people use kerosene in cleaning is because it's a petroleum distillate and acts as a solvent on many oil-based soils. However, kerosene *itself* is a light oil, and leaves an oily residue behind. Besides, unless it's scented it has an unpleasant odor that permeates porous substances—kerosene is undesirable as a cleaner for that reason alone. The inconvenience of finding and storing it is another minus for using kerosene to clean. If you need a volatile solvent cleaner for removing oily soils, I recommend dry-cleaning solvent, turpentine, or even paint thinner. Most kerosene recommendations are a carryover from old wives' tales of 1880 when it was the best thing available for some cleaning situations—this is the 1990s!

IS IT TRUE THAT YOU CAN TELL A COUPLE'S RELATIONSHIP BY LOOKING IN THEIR REFRIGERATOR?

How come everyone in the world heard me make that statement? But all said in jest—or parable—has meaning, so here goes . . .

I'm a firm believer in a principle called *carryover*. In plainer words, the personal characteristics you exhibit in one situation are essentially the same ones you will show in other, totally unrelated situations. A person who's sloppy in appearance will generally be sloppy in speech, promise-keeping, and gardening. If you are an aggressive competitor on the tennis court, you generally will be that way in PTA meetings, golf, fruit canning, and style of dress.

The refrigerator is probably the most personal of all furniture and appliances—behind its door (and often in front of it!) is a composite picture of your organization, judgment, decisions, hopes, failures, and successes. It's not open to the world (Remember how upset you are when anyone outside the family looks in your fridge?) but *you* can tell a lot by taking a hard look in it.

Are you the type who lets the refrigerator go and go and go, cramming in more and more and finally going to two-story stacking, ignoring spills and vegetables that have shrivelled beyond identification—then suddenly in a dedicated attack of repentance you whip into it, leaving it gleaming and immaculate? You are probably also letting relationships or living strains and irritations go, go, go, until they are intolerable—then in a big weeping, soul-cleansing trauma, you sweep your cowering family into a confrontation, followed by a tearful kissy-pie all-is-well. But then you start stacking the fridge again, putting lids on the problems that you'd rather delay making decisions on. You do this until the fridge (or family situation) stinks and is ready to explode—and then you dive in again and make peace, love, apologies, promises, etc.

Those who keep their refrigerators bare (I mean not a morsel to snack on—not a saucer of cold peaches or a peeled boiled egg in there) often have empty, cold relationships with family and associates.

The person who can't manage to put a lid on a smelly container in the refrigerator probably can't keep the lid on a neighborhood secret.

If you have disguised or hidden "no-nos" (fattening chocolates) stashed in secret places in your fridge, you'll probably have other hidden things (gifts, rash purchases, damaged things, spare money) the rest of the family doesn't know about.

If a fridge is dominated by processed foodstuffs, it generally signifies the time the family spends together is limited.

If the fridge is dominated by the husband's "habit" residue (liquor, fish bait, film), that generally means the woman of the house is far from liberated (equal).

Before any of you sit back and feel too smug, the same diagnoses can be made from toolboxes, lockers at school, scout knapsacks, etc.

HOW DO I CARE FOR MY ROCK OR TILE ENTRYWAY?

Rock, brick, ceramic, "Mexican," quarry, and assorted earth tiles are extremely durable flooring materials, and can be kept looking good with a minimum of care. To illustrate my point, I'll ask you to recall the "rock" tile floors in the large shopping malls you've undoubtedly patronized. Did the floor look dull, dry and scuffed? Probably not. In most malls, the floors are kept clean and glowing to present a positive image to the customers. The owners, expecting thousands of people a day to be walking up and down the broad thoroughfares, choose flooring noted for its durability and ease of maintenance. When you compare the mall's traffic to that in your entryway (thirty or forty per day, maybe) there's no reason your floor can't look bright and shiny all the time.

You can keep rock floors looking "rustic" (like the lodge's) or highly polished ("downtown"). Some rock or tile *has* to have a finish applied to its naturally dull or porous surface. The proper finish not only seals and smooths out the surface, it also deepens and brings out the natural colors and beauty of the stone or tile. If you have a problem tile or rock floor, most likely the problem lies in your choice of finish products and their application. Many people, suffering from the no-wax floor syndrome, make the mistake of putting a varnish-type finish on their floors, and expect it to last forever. The finish looks great for a while, but eventually ends up scabbing and peeling like a sunburned back. The secret lies in putting down a permanent, penetrating sealer, topped with a renewable finish material (to *keep* it looking good).

The sealer can be of the easy-to-use water emulsion type or a resinous product, but in any case it should be a *penetrating* sealer. You want your sealer to penetrate and seal—not leave a thick film on top of the stone. Sealers are very hard and brittle, and if you have a thick layer of sealer on top of your stone, it will tend to chip off and peel just like the varnish does. After proper sealing, apply several coats of a good floor finish to protect the base coat and to give the desired smoothness and gloss. This can be a liquid acrylic finish like you use on your vinyl floors, or a paste wax. Waxes and other finishes are softer than the sealer, and thus should not chip or peel. They will *wear* off, though! The finish coat must be renewed from time to time to maintain its beauty, and should not be allowed to wear down to the seal coat. The finish can be stripped off and reapplied without removing the sealer.

After your entry floor is properly finished and looking great, don't forget to put down a good entry mat (see p. 104) to protect the heavy traffic portion just inside the door, and to keep the grit off. These mats are now available in nice earth tones and decorator colors to enhance the beauty of your natural stone or tile floor.

HOW DO YOU CLEAN TVs AND STEREOS?

Dust is sound equipment's (and computer's) worst enemy, and amplifiers and other high-current components attract it because they are electrically charged.

Dust damages tape heads, needles and cartridges, screens, switches, keyboards and connectors.

I use a dry disposable Masslinn dustcloth 80% of the time. This should take care of the surface dust. Remember to keep the cover on your turntable! Periodic vacuuming of ventilation louvers and foam or mesh speaker grills will keep your components looking good—and operating coolly.

When you must clean off the hand oils, smudges, and spots on your TV screen or other components, a cloth dampened with a neutral cleaner solution followed with a dry towel buffing is best. I'd keep spray polishes and cleaners away from any set I cared for if I were you. And don't forget to unplug them while you clean!

Q80

HOW DO YOU CLEAN THE TRACKS OF SHOWER AND PATIO DOORS, MEDICINE CABINETS, ETC.?

Any door mounted on a base (bottom) track will someday cause a problem. The wear of rollers and tracks is accelerated by the dirt buildup and water runoff from the windows and doors. Moisture turns the accumulated dirt into a gummy residue that "freezes" or binds up rollers when the residue gets hard.

The solution is simple—clean and maintain tracks *regularly*. That means don't wait until the doors are beginning to stick; vacuuming them then does little good because anything loose is quickly ground into gummy stuff. Take a spray bottle of all-purpose cleaner solution (see p. 46), squirt all over and inside the track and rollers, and let it set to dissolve hard "gummys." Then wrap a screwdriver with a terrycloth or similar rag and wipe out the gunk (the cloth must have some body to it—silk, thin cotton, or linen rags work poorly for this purpose). It's a little awkward, but a couple of passes and the track will clean up. If the track is kept clean, the roller stays clean and operable.

Generally I wouldn't lubricate tracks with graphite, petroleum jelly, or oil because this will increase gunk buildup. In general, I advise two things:

1. Get top roller tracks instead of bottom tracks if you have a choice next time—and buy the best you can.
2. Keep them clean.

I'D REALLY LIKE TO KNOW IF MEN ARE DOING MORE HOUSEWORK THAN THEY USED TO (AND THAT WASN'T VERY MUCH).

I'm sorry to tell you it *still* isn't very much. I've collected thousands upon thousands of comment cards on which I asked, "How much cleaning is done by spouse and children?" The answers even in this day of "liberation" and "sexual equality" and two career households, are pathetic. When I was in London on a book tour once, a little poll the B.B.C. did right on the air, did a lot to explain why the "latest study" of how much housework men do, never seems to quite jibe with life as we know it on the homefront. A group of British men was asked how much of the housework they did. Most said, "about 50%." When the wives of those same men were asked, they doubled over with laughter—5% was closer.

It isn't fair, it isn't right, it isn't even *moral*—but cleaning as we know it has generally fallen to the woman's lot and that seems to still be true.

Think a minute. Where did you—or anybody— learn to clean? You can go to school and learn to sew, play a horn, dribble a ball, operate on a frog, split an atom, identify historical characters and 10,000 other edifying, useful things. But where did you learn to clean? From your mother—and she learned from her mother, who learned from her mother, who learned from her mother, who learned from her mother (who even made her own soap and underwear). Way back it was established that the man hunted, fished, and brought home the food, and the woman gathered wood and cleaned up after all three (wood, food, and man). Along with the tradition of how and what to clean came down *who* should clean (the woman), and people are still being taught—by their mothers.

Everyone in the family participates in big Sunday dinners, tag football, popcorn in front of the TV, welcoming guests, or working on a Cub Scout or 4-H project. We LOVE it, that's living! But when it's all over, there sits a four-foot stack of dishes that you've done hundreds of times before and will do hundreds more . . . there is the pile of muddy, grass-stained jerseys and sweatsuits. The rug (which you've vacuumed thirty times this month) is strewn with popcorn—greasy bowls everywhere, left lying where they were finished. Forgotten belongings (that you'll have to box and mail) and dirty sheets and towels greet you after the visitors have said good-bye. Bits of papier-mâché, beads, and feathers from Cub Scout masks are glued to the sunporch floor. This is housework—it isn't progressive, only restorative, getting back to where you started.

Housework is hard work because it receives minor (if any) appreciation: all evidence of accomplishment is washed down the drain or chucked in the dumpster. Where there is no glory, no status, no lasting evidence of achievement, it is only natural to dislike hard, drudging activity. It's not so much the physical work of housework, but the amount of a lifetime spent doing "invisible" things that embitters people. Doing the same chores over and over is discouraging. It's accepted that housework always "has to be done" and "somebody has to do it"—and we know who that "somebody" is. Constantly working hard just to be back where you started is not a fair burden to place on one person. This can be changed by reducing the need to clean; designing work away; preventing dirt and junk from entering the house; getting a few good tools that will do the job better; using a few professional secrets to cut corners—and above all, getting those who "dirty up" to clean up behind themselves. People can learn (before they go out on their own, when they'll *have* to) that housework isn't done by disembodied forces (*someone* has to deal with the stuff they drop in the hamper and forget).

Cleaning is everyone's job! Anyone old enough to mess up is old enough to clean up. Cleaning is no more a woman's job than anyone else's, and anyone who makes a mother, wife, grandmother, or secretary clean up after him (or her) is a simple fink!

Q 82

I HAVE AN OLD HOME WITH DARK, YELLOWED HARDWOOD FLOORS. SHALL I SAND THEM OFF?

I like those old hardwood floors. They look nice and rich and warm, and they *can* be easy to keep up. The yellowing and darkness you see is most likely the buildup of coats of varnish applied to the floor in the past: that old varnish is on there harder and thicker than you think. The old wax or finish will have to come off before you can make the floor look young, fresh, and revitalized. I wouldn't sand it off—it will be a mess and the old varnish will glaze and plug your expensive sanding belt, almost instantly rendering it ineffective. And reducing the thickness of the wood, even a little, will weaken the floor's structural strength, reduce durability, and cause it to buckle and squeak. You all remember the old hardwood floor in the school gym, where it was the duty of the custodian to sand and refinish it every summer. After a few years of sanding, the floor got too thin, started to warp and arch, and was hard to maintain.

Instead of sanding off that ugly old darkened finish, buy some paint and varnish remover and, according to directions, apply it generously to the floor. The remover will instantly loosen and "skim up" the finish to a point where it can be scraped up and removed. If the varnish is many coats thick, you might have to apply another coat of remover in places where it doesn't completely lift off the old finish. (The remover won't hurt the wood.) Let the floor dry and sweep off any dried flaky residue that may remain. I'd then hire or rent a floor buffer with a 000 sanding screen disc (it looks like a window screen). When applied to the floor, it smooths the surface, knocking off the old lap edges from previous applications and the rest of the dried varnish and varnish remover. Your floor should be lighter now (unless the original owner stained it). Don't sweat the small nicks and scratches. I know you want it to look like the piano or dresser top, but it won't because you don't walk on piano or dresser tops. When the new finish is on, it will look good—or at least, "antique." (Some antique floor fanatics beat up their floors on purpose!)

Ask a good local paint store what is the best clear protective finish available for your type of floor. Follow directions! Be sure to get all the dust and remover off before applying the finish. These finishes are extremely easy to apply. I'd thin the first coat a little (about one cup of thinner per gallon or according to the thinning suggestions on the label) so the finish will penetrate down into the wood; if you don't the finish will hang as a sheet on top of the floor and chip more easily. Apply a generous second coat. Two coats generally do an older floor because age has made it hard, which retards its absorbing powers. After a week or so I'd wax it and treat it like other floors. Keep gravel and other foot traffic debris off it. Use good mats at the entrance of the house (see p. 104) and don't roll that piano over it; wheel tracks is one design you don't need in your nice wood floor.

Q83

MY FIBERGLASS SHOWER IS IMPOSSIBLE. HOW DO I CLEAN IT?

Fiberglass and other plastic materials are now being used extensively to make inexpensive, lightweight tub and shower enclosures and shower doors. Builders often use these units because they are less costly than conventional porcelain or ceramic tile units, and because they are easier to install. Unfortunately, they often require more maintenance than the glazed finishes it replaces, and is more easily damaged. With proper care, however, it can look good and be quite serviceable.

The basic thing to remember about fiberglass is to avoid damaging it, thereby making it more difficult to clean. Don't use abrasive cleansers or scouring pads, as these will roughen the surface and make dirt cling harder. Strong oxidizers such as bleach, harsh acids, and volatile solvents can also damage the finish. If your soap scum problem can't be eliminated by regular cleaning with a disinfectant cleaner, I recommend that you wax the unit when new, or clean your old one up, wax it, and keep it waxed to ease cleaning. Products containing silicone (such as Armorall or silicone glaze) should not be used on the floor unless you want to practice skiing in your shower. Most auto paste waxes can be used on the floor of shower units without making them slick, but try any wax you intend to use on the walls first.

If you clean your fiberglass shower weekly, a mild phosphoric acid cleaner should do the trick and a white nylon scrub sponge can be used without scratching. For heavy soap scum, using it full-strength is okay if you rinse it off right away.

If you have a fiberglass unit that has been scoured and scratched, auto rubbing compound will polish it up again, and a good wax job should make it look like new. The secret is to keep it maintained and don't let the soap scum build up until it's a major operation.

HOW DO I CLEAN MY FIREPLACE?

When homemakers ask this question, they're usually referring to the exterior face of the unit, not the firebox and interior damper. A fireplace probably has more aesthetic appeal than energy or money-saving value, so those 95% of fireplaces with soot-blackened, grimy fronts cause owners not a little discomfort. Unsuccessful attempts to clean these often leave the face looking worse than before, and impossible to ever get clean, so be cautious. (See pp. 112–13 re cleaning brick.)

Before you baptize it with gallons of chemicals and liquids, check the surface. If your fireplace is constructed of light, soft sandstone or stark white unsealed brick, moisture will drive stains and dirt deeper into the surface. If the stone is an oakley flagstone or extremely hard non-porous masonry, then you can just get a bucket of degreaser solution and a good stiff-bristled brush and go at it. After the grime has all oozed out, spray-rinse with clear water (using a spray bottle or a common garden sprayer) and use some terry toweling to absorb the runoff.

If you have a soft, porous surface and a ten-year accumulation of crud, you probably aren't going to get it sparkling clean, because time, humidity, heat, etc., have already locked in the dirt film. Sometimes it's best to just leave it, and call it rustic!

My first advice about cleaning any fireplace is to vacuum it with a small hand brush attachment, then go over it with a dry sponge. (See p. 24.) If you now determine it is washable, scrub away; if not, I'd leave it. Or sandblast it or paint it. Yup! Bricks painted with a white eggshell enamel look sharp and can be cleaned easily. Whatever you do, don't try to clean your fireplace with a bricklayer's muriatic acid bath (like your "expert" neighbor suggested). Acid baths are effective on new brick because they break down the chemical binders in any left behind mortar drips, but on old dirty, greasy, dingy bricks they are relatively helpless. Half-cleaned bricks look worse than uncleaned ones. If mortar joints look bad, I always paint mine with an opaque colored stain—it goes on quickly and accents the stone or brick nicely.

I'VE CLEANED SPOTS OUT OF MY CARPETS AND ZAP, THEY REAPPEAR IN THE SAME PLACE!

TICK
TICK

The return of spots is as frustrating as cutting weeds and having them pop up again. The solution to your carpet spot is the same as the way you keep weeds from reappearing. If you totally remove a weed, it won't return. If you get *all* the spot out of the carpet, no spot will return. Spots "return" because of a process known as wicking. Remember how a lamp wick moves kerosene up the wick to burn? Well, when most carpet spots are treated (only on the surface), the spot disappears, it looks good, and the happy spotter leaves. Then moisture helps the stain residue deep in the carpet roots and backing "wick up" through the fiber and dries on the top—and the carpet looks almost as bad as it did originally.

Any soap or cleaner residue left in the carpet leaves a sticky surface that attracts dirt; this is another reason "removed" spots reappear in the same place. Be sure to remove *all* the stain and *all* the soap residue when you clean up a spot. (See the stain removal steps and specific stain removers in *Is There Life After Housework?*) Remember, even if you can't see it, it's there, so keep working and absorbing and rinsing longer than you think you need to, until your clean white absorbing cloth shows no evidence of stain.

On carpet and upholstery, after it's cleaned, put a thick pad of toweling over the spot, weight it down with books, and leave it there for several hours to "wick up" any remaining moisture into the towel. This will eliminate the reappearing "ring."

I HEAR WARNINGS ABOUT SERIOUS ACCIDENTS WHILE CLEANING—HOW COULD IT BE DANGEROUS TO CLEAN?

Nobody pays much attention to home accidents until they have one. Then they run around with a swollen eye, acid burns, or pinched fingers and spread scary tales. More than half of all accidents happen in and around the home; hundreds of thousands of them are directly connected with home cleaning or maintenance, because this is when people use unfamiliar chemicals, climb higher than they usually do, lift new and heavier objects, work when they are tired, or get so enthused with "progress" and getting finished that they forget to watch their step, or where they set the paint bucket. I could tell you all sorts of gory stories, but thought a simple visual checklist might do a better job of preventing you from having to tell your story of how you survived a ladder fall.

HOW CAN IT BE DANGEROUS TO CLEAN?

Falls account for a high percentage of home accidents. Choosing stuff to stand on is no place to use your imagination—use only approved stepladders and scaffolding.

Keep water away from electrical outlets.

Overloading electrical circuits is a major cause of fires.

Never reach under a beater-bar vacuum to see if the beater is working.

Don't store stuff on the steps.

In the mood for a real shocker? Grab an old, frayed electrical cord with wet hands.

Don't set the bucket at the foot of the ladder.

Get help lifting heavy objects. Next to falls, lifting injuries are the most common.

Sloppy storage can be dangerous.

Make sure your ladder is set at a safe angle and firmly anchored. When you use a ladder, angle 1 foot from wall for every 4 feet of height. Never stand on top rung.

Be careful how you store and mix cleaning chemicals—many are caustic and poisonous.

Sweep it up—don't pick it up!

To avoid slips and falls, rubber-soled shoes are the safest to use while cleaning.

Don't wring out mops with your hands—all mop heads pick up glass, pins, needles, toothpicks, and other sharp objects.

Move the bucket *before* you move the ladder.

Move heavy items the right way—with a cloth slipped underneath them.

HOW DO I CLEAN VELVET?

Velvet wears well, but is a higher maintenance material than most furniture covers. Velvets are difficult to clean, and it's generally not a home project. Having them professionally dry-cleaned is the best way to go. Cotton velvet and velvet drapes of any description should always be sent to the cleaners—let *them* sweat it. Synthetic velvet you could shampoo yourself; the little tags on the furniture will identify the material. If the tags are gone, ask a furniture distributor, retailer, or professional cleaner.

With the exception of crushed synthetic, velvet is not a very practical material to have around. The nap wear exaggerates worn spots. Any velvet (except crushed) will look bad if portions of the nap become matted or lie the wrong way. You can use a damp cloth to brush the nap up so it all stands uniform, but that's time-consuming.

Velvet is easier to enjoy in clothes than in furniture. (Which would you really rather have, a velvet chair to gaze upon or a snuggly velvet robe?) Bear this in mind when you're ogling that luxurious velvet love seat—and if you must go velvet, remember that whites, yellows, and golds are tough to keep up; browns, reds, and greens help minimize problems.

WHAT IS THE BEST WAY TO CLEAN SHOWER CURTAINS?

If you've tried cleaning them in place (generally called the bathtub wrestling match) or laying them out on the rug or lawn (generally called stupid), you know that's not the way to go. A warm, gentle setting on the washing machine with a little ammonia or even bleach added to your detergent (to beat the soap/mineral buildup) is the wise way to go at it.

There are a few kinds that you can't throw in your washer—check the label, or the washer after you're through, and the answer will be clear. Remember that shower curtains are inexpensive, considering the amount of use they get—so consider replacement when they start looking shabby. Best of all is to eliminate them (*and* shower doors) like I'm doing in the maintenance-free house I'm building.

SHOULD YOU WASH WALLS AND CEILINGS BEFORE PAINTING?

Only if they need it! The prime reason for precleaning is to get paint to bond well to the old surface. Paint won't adhere well to dirt, grease, oils, cobwebs, spitballs, or sticky foodstuff-laden walls, so most walls should be cleaned in some way before painting.

If the wall is greasy, wash it with a strong heavy-duty cleaner solution. A wall with only mild age and wear can be dusted down and painted, or quickly swipe it down with a dry sponge. Stains and marks will probably be covered by the paint.

Some things that often do need to be removed are the specks, roller lint, and hair that stuck in the last coat of paint. You can't wash *that* off. A quick whish over the surface with fine sandpaper will have an amazing effect on the adherence and looks of the finished job especially on woodwork. If you are in doubt about some marks, such as felt pen marks, ballpoint pen ink and the like, slap a thin coat of clear shellac over them before painting—it will seal them off.

If cleaning seems impossible in some textures or situations, talk to your trusty paint store expert—there are special primers and sealers that can deal with about any kind of surface.

DON, DO YOU THINK IT'S IMMORAL TO HAVE A MAID?

Sounds like a loaded question. I left this question just like it was asked because deciding to get a "maid" (whether or not to get help with the housework) is often more of a "moral" than a financial issue. The question really should have been "Do you think it's wrong to get someone else to do your cleaning?"

The answer is simple—no. I think it's great to get someone else to help around the house, if you need it. We all use professional help with the things we can't, won't, or don't want to do (transportation, making or dry-cleaning clothes, preparing our food, making corsages, styling our hair, selling our homes, teaching our children, fixing our plumbing). All of these we *could* do ourselves, but for various reasons we find it more intelligent, economical, convenient, or satisfying to pay someone else to do it. None of these things—which we delegate without a second thought every day and week of our lives—is any more skilled or personal than waxing floors, shampooing carpet, or cleaning high light fixtures. Many people have physical conditions (such as allergies) or emotional hangups (fear of heights, noise, bugs, etc.) that make cleaning a horror. Others entertain constantly and have ten times their share of cleaning, or they work a full-time job outside the home. I'm a well-known professional cleaner, yet I have someone else clean my office because he does it well, has more time than I do, and needs a job. So I feel good about it. Getting professional or outside help *is* the smart—"moral"—even admirable—thing to do.

I'm a professional cleaner; that's what a maid is. "We" do work where/when people can't justify or handle doing it themselves. If you don't really need a maid, but just have to have one for prestige, that's fine, too—it's a lot cheaper than a psychiatrist. We maids like to improve the mental as well as the physical quality of a home.

Once people use professional help they usually find it is much more useful and far less expensive than membership in a spa or twenty extra gadgets on an automobile! Yes, it's totally "moral" to have a maid. . . .

HOW MUCH WOULD IT COST TO HAVE MY HOME CLEANED PROFESSIONALLY?

That depends on whether you own Dracula's castle, an 8' × 28' mobile home, or a studio apartment/condo. It also depends on what you define as "cleaned." I can give you a ballpark estimate on the two categories (1992 prices):

CLEANED I

Maid Work

Ordinary vacuuming, dusting, polishing, spot cleaning, sweeping—mopping, wax touch up—bathroom cleaning, watering plants, etc.:

Large Home ....$40-$60 per time

Average Home ....$35-$50 per time

Tiny Home ....$25-$30 per time

(if the cleaner uses his or her own equipment, add $5 per visit)

CLEANED II

Professional Cleaning Crew

When a cleaning crew goes through the entire home washing all walls, windows, and woodwork, waxing floors, shampooing carpet and upholstery:

5,000 sq. ft. Big Fancy Home ......$1000 and up

4,000 sq. ft. Big Home $890

1,800 sq. ft. Average Home $550

1,100 sq. ft. Small Home $385

800 sq. ft. Average Apt. $300

Average local travel costs and preparation time are already figured into these costs.

Variables

The state of the local labor market, age of the home and its general condition, type of furnishings, wall and floor coverings, number of knickknacks, etc., make a difference. Location makes a *big* difference. An average-size home 75 miles out in the desert from Las Vegas would probably cost more (considering travel time and vehicle use) than a big fancy home in the city. Dusty weather conditions, hard water deposits on chrome and windows, and other environmental factors influence the cost, too.

Get a bid! There are tons of pro cleaners and the ones that "know" their business will know exactly what it will cost and can tell you to the penny. Then you can decide.

I HAVE FOUR BOYS WHO MISS THE TOILET; WHAT SHALL I DO?

Keep out of the way! Painting a red dot as a target near the bottom of the back of the toilet bowl will present an irresistible challenge. Signs that help create a hero-identification situation also help dry up careless behavior. And making them clean up their own mess with disinfectant cleaner solution—make sure they get around the base of the toilet and floor area—will improve accuracy 70%.

Try these tactics and treat them nice and they will "aim to please!"

Q 93

IF I'M GOING INTO HOUSECLEANING PROFESSIONALLY, HOW MUCH AM I WORTH?

It all depends on how much work you can do in a given amount of time, in a professional manner. Certain jobs have a certain value, but your personal efficiency and technical skill are also important—how valuable you are will ultimately depend on how fast and well you can do the job. Most people could make $10-$25 per hour once they have gained true "professional status" in the housecleaning field. True pro status comes through:

1. **Experience:** Having faced and handled many different types of cleaning challenges—as well as the many types of *people* you have to deal with as a cleaner. Your confidence and competence will develop from experience.

2. **Study:** Seeking and reading written material, attending training sessions and seminars, keeping up with new products and methods will all help you to be an efficient cleaner.

3. **Long hours of hard work:** A cleaning business is not a 9-to-5 job. You clean during "off" hours and lots of them. When competition keeps prices low, more hours of time have to be spent.

Don't work for an hourly wage; everyone is in the habit of thinking a cleaner ought to get minimum wage and if you ask for an hourly rate higher than that, most customers' faces turn white. Instead, submit a bid for the work the customer has in mind (see the table on page 198 of *Is There Life After Housework?*). Tell the customer, "I'll wash all your windows and clean the blinds for $67.50." They like that because they know the cost, with no surprises; you can then work hard, fast, and efficiently, and do it in 5 hours and make $17.37 per hour. You have to charge enough to cover more than your time. Remember: you have the expenses of a phone, vehicle, gas, supplies, and equipment that will wear out. Occasionally you'll break or ruin something or even underbid a job or two.

Professional cleaning is a good direction to go. Here are some addresses of other technical authorities where you may inquire about cleaning career opportunities, professional training, sources of professional supplies, technique and material updates, etc. The following ought to be able to supply almost any cleaning information you want.

1. Building Service Contractors Association
   10201 Lee Highway, Ste 225
   Fairfax, VA 22030
2. *Cleaning Management Institute*
   13 Century Hill Drive
   Latham, NY 12110
3. Cleaning Center
   P.O. Box 39
   Pocatello, ID 83204

IS IT PRACTICAL TO OWN MY OWN CARPET-SHAMPOOING EQUIPMENT?

Almost never! Many people who own or rent a 3,000-square foot carpeted house or apartment figure they are in the big time and need to own their own carpet-cleaning equipment. It looks practical on paper, because shampooing 5,000 feet of carpet (at 1992 prices, 12¢ per square foot) is $600 annually. For $800 to $1,500 you could get your own hot water extractor unit, which would last for years.

You'll be sorry if you take the step. *First,* with good matting (see p. 104) you won't have to shampoo annually, maybe once every 3-5 years. *Second,* if you watch for a professional carpet cleaning sale you can get your carpets cleaned for 8-10¢ per square foot. *Third,* all this equipment (unit, hose, cord, wands, spotting kits, and so on) will take a heap of storage area. *Fourth,* carpet extraction equipment is a high-maintenance item—it breaks and gets out of adjustment easily, and will depreciate rapidly if not used and serviced regularly (and we aren't a service society any more). *Fifth,* every neighbor, relative, friend, and even carpet cleaner will find out that you have the unit and not only expect to borrow it, but feel slighted if you don't accompany it and do the job. (Borrowers are the true kiss of death to good carpet equipment.) *Sixth,* the carpet-cleaning chemical costs, and also has to be picked up and stored. *Seventh* is the work. The equipment looks neat and will do wonderful things, but running and lifting carpet equipment (and heaving furniture around) is gut-hard, skilled work—it requires not only a strong back but knowledge of color, fabric, moisture control, spotting, etc. In a few cases it's a good idea, but for 98% of us, no!

HOW DO YOU GET THOSE LITTLE "NON-SKID" DESIGN STICK-'EMS OFF THE BOTTOM OF A TUB?

Remove as much of the solid material as you can by scraping (using a razor blade in a holder and keeping it wet with soapy water), then use acetone, or nail polish remover or De-Solv-it to remove the adhesive residue. But remember, they were put there to keep people from slipping in a wet tub—even if they look a little shabby, they still work (and who besides the family looks in your tub?)

HOW IS LINSEED OIL AS A CLEANER?

Poor! Linseed oil is a wood preservative/conditioner (commonly called a penetrant), not a wood finish. Linseed oil is primarily used to protect dry, unfinished wood from nature's elements. But most of the people who want to use linseed oil in the home try to use it on varnished wood surfaces, which does no good—the oil never benefits the wood, since it can't penetrate varnish. When linseed oil doesn't penetrate but just remains on the surface, it stays tacky/sticky for a long time. I only use linseed oil on shingle roofs, my log cabins, and shovel and pick handles, to keep them from splitting from exposure to weather.

If you need a penetrant for exterior wood conditioning, you can buy it at a paint store. If you must use linseed oil, use boiled linseed oil—it dries and doesn't leave a tacky surface.

DON, DO YOU HELP YOUR WIFE AROUND THE HOUSE?

Yes. Like many other men who claim authority, I run things around our house. . . .

Said "things" include, but are not limited to, the following: the vacuum cleaner, dishwasher, lawnmower, window squeegee, toilet plunger, carpet shampooer, paint roller, garbage compacter, waffle iron, taxi service, mop bucket, oven, brooms, sprinkler, hose, dustcloth, etc. . . .

Seriously, though, indoors I shampoo the carpet; wash walls, paint and remodel; install, replace and wash mats and light fixtures, troubleshoot, etc.; my wife does most of the routine housecleaning. I also do the outside stuff like knocking down hornets' nests and cleaning the garage.

Although we keep things clean, we use our house hard and don't get excited if a fly dies in a window track. We live fairly simply—I think fancy cooking is a waste of time and over-decorated houses are a pain.

I do keep the house equipped with good tools, new efficient machines, and the best cleaning chemicals—the material and equipment necessary to minimize housework for all of us. I also bring in professionals from my company when extra help is needed, who seem to do a better job for my wife than they do for "The Boss's."

HOW DO I GET PAINT AND OTHER HARD SPECKS OFF WINDOWS?

I assume you mean dried paint from either brush lap or paint gun overspray. Ninety percent of window glass is smooth and hard enough to scrape (but be sure not to try to scrape Plexiglas). The scrape system works great on labels or window decorations you wish to remove, as well as on paint. Always use a new razor blade in a scraper holder—don't use it loose by itself because you'll have less control. Don't use the plastic windshield scraper you got at the service station—it's fine for scraping frost, etc., but a car windshield is different from house glass.

Before you start scraping, wet the window with soapy water—this lubricates the razor and helps loosen and release specks from the surface for easy removal. When scraping with the razor blade, *go in only one direction: FORWARD.* Dragging a razor back over the window does nothing to remove anything—but it will trap sand, grit, mortar specks, old hard paint flakes or whatever under the blade and often scratch or damage the glass.

You can dissolve paint with paint removers but this is messy and often gets on the sill (where you don't want the paint removed!). But dissolving is about the only way to go on rough-textured windows. Don't leave any slop marks or streaks of remover on the window; they will harden and be almost as tough to get off as the paint was. Wash and squeegee the window after you finish! (See Chapter 9 of *Is There Life After Housework?*)

HOW DO I GO ABOUT DEJUNKING A HOME AFTER LIVING THERE FOR TWENTY-SEVEN YEARS—AND BEING A PACK RAT FOR FIFTY?

Move! Have a sale, have a fire, donate it to charity, or (if the stuff was already old when you got it) open an antique shop! Don't love anything that can't love you back—that JUNK is robbing you of all kinds of time and energy, and if you aren't using it, what good is it doing you? It for sure isn't impressing or benefiting anyone.

Must junk served its purpose before it was salted away (like shipping boxes, used wrapping paper, defunct wristwatches, old tires, worn faucets, old schoolbooks and 1,000 more shelf-sitters)—you don't *really* need it, do you? Dejunking a home, office, shop, etc., will do as much for you mentally as it will to save cleaning time: every piece of junk stashed away or hidden (discreetly or indiscreetly) is also stashed away in your mind and is subconsciously taking a toll of your emotional, spiritual, and physical resources. Once discarded, it is discarded from your mind, and you are free from keeping mental tabs on it.

Another burden junk thrusts on us is that we feel obligated to use it whether we need it or not. If we don't use it, then we worry about why we have it at all. Junk will get you—all fifty years of it—don't sit there and argue that it won't!

Recommended reading: (In fact the greatest stress relieving gift you'll give to yourself all year.)

Not For Packrats Only (Plume)

Clutter's Last Stand (Writer's Digest)

IS IT WORTH IT?

Sure it is! That's why you haven't given up before now. Have you noticed that as you improve the speed and quality of your housework, other areas of your life seem to improve? It's called carryover. Cleaning and organizing a house is one of life's best seminars in self-improvement. You "absorb" more lessons than a sponge, you're uplifted even as you lift the grime from the garage floor.

The cleanliness level in your house projects your growing pride in yourself. The discipline and care with which you remove the dust and cobwebs from the corners of your rooms will carry over into a desire to wipe the cobwebs from the corners of your personality. One of housework's greatest values is its ability to build you into an efficient, appealing person!

A clean house can and will get messed up again, but you can't mess up the improvements in quality of life your efforts have produced. How you live in and care for your dwelling shapes your personality—and your destiny. Home is the center of civilization. So it's got to be worth it. *It IS worth it!*

THE TOOLS TALKED ABOUT IN THIS BOOK

These are the tools the professionals use. I introduced them to the homemaker in 1981, and you couldn't tear them away now. It's easy to understand why. They do a faster and better job, and cost less in the long run, too.

Where can you get them? Where the pros do—at the janitorial-supply store. Just look in the Yellow Pages under "J." If you'd find it easier to order them by mail, send a **postcard** with you name and address to Clean Report, P.O. Box 700, Pocatello, ID 83204 and they'll be happy to send you a catalog.

Mats. Professional "walkoff" mats for inside and outside  the door. **Inside** you want nylon or olefin pile with vinyl or rubber backing. **Outside** you want something more textured such as synthetic turf on a nonskid backing. 3' × 5' or 3' × 6' is a good size.

Glass Cleaner. The pro version of a "Windex" type  cleaner you can mix up yourself inexpensively from concentrate. For spray cleaning small windowpanes, mirrors, appliances, chrome. Available in gallon jugs or premeasured packets.

Spray Bottle. Sturdy transparent plastic with a trigger- spray head. Pro-quality spray bottles perform better and last longer and come in 22 oz. and quart size.

Disinfectant Cleaner. A general-purpose cleaner with serious germ-killing ability, for anyplace in the home that needs sanitizing or deodorizing. A "quaternary" is the kind you want. Available as concentrate.

Neutral All-Purpose Cleaner. A gentle but effective cleaner that will handle most of the household cleaning we do. Available as concentrate in gallon jugs or premeasured packets.

White Nylon Scrub Sponge. A regular cellulose sponge on one side, white nylon mesh on the other. My all-around favorite cleaning tool. Enables you to get tough with dirt whenever you need to as you're cleaning along, without taking a chance of scratching things. 3M makes a good one.

Heavy-Duty Cleaner/Degreaser. A meaner cleaner for when you're up against greasy or stubborn soil. Available as concentrate in gallon jugs or premeasured packets.

Wax Stripper. Commercial strength, nonammoniated.

Cleaning Cloth. The pro cleaner's secret weapon, for quick streak-free drying, polishing, wiping, and mild scrubbing. Made from cotton terrycloth in an ingenious design that gives you 16 fresh surfaces to work with. Available from The Cleaning Center.

Dust Mop. You want a 14" or 18" pro model with a cotton head and a swivel handle.

"Wax" or Floor Finish. A "22-25% solid, self-polishing, non-buffable" such as Top Gloss.

Masslinn Cloth. A disposable paper "cloth" that's chemically treated to catch and hold dust. It also leaves a nice non-oily low luster on furniture.

Upright Vacuum. For speed, maneuverability and pickup power on carpeting, these can't be beat. A commercial model such as the Eureka Sanitaire has a stronger motor, beater bar and bag, a longer cord, and more durable and easily replaceable parts all over.

Oil Soap. A true soap (as opposed to the detergents we mostly clean with today) made from vegetable oil. It's mild enough to clean wood surfaces safely, and the little bit of oil it leaves behind on the surface will be buffed by your drying towel to a handsome sheen.

Electrostatic Dustcloth. Dustcloths such as the Dust Bunny and New Pig made of special fabric that attracts and holds dust by static electricity. When they're laden with dust they can be laundered and reused.

Squeegee. To do a first-class job you need a pro-quality brass squeegee such as the Ettore. A 12″ blade is best for most home size windows; for picture windows and the like you might want to go to 14″ or larger.

Lambswool Duster. A large puff of wool on a long handle, that does high and low dusting with ease. You can also run it across detailed and convoluted surfaces like fancy picture frames, woodwork, and bookcases, and it will reach in and gently pull off the dust without disturbing anything. The natural oil and static attraction of the wool is the secret.

Bowl Swab with bowl caddy. A "bunny tail" of cotton, rayon, or acrylic on a plastic handle. Used for applying bowl cleaner to a toilet, and for coaxing all of the water out of the bowl first so the cleaner can work full strength.

Dry Sponge. A disposable 5" × 7" pad of soft rubber used to "dry clean" surface dirt and smoke from painted walls, paneling, ceilings, wallpaper, etc.

Phosphoric Acid Cleaner. For removing mineral or "lime" scale. The 8 or 9% solution you can get at janitorial-supply stores (you don't want anything stronger than that for home use) will work much faster than supermarket delimers.

Bacteria/Enzyme Digester. A culture of live, beneficial bacteria that you mix up to digest organic materials like vomit and urine that cause persistent and hard to remove stains and odors. Outright Pet Odor Eliminator is one good brand.

Pet Rake. A tool specially designed to deal with the exasperating problem of pet hair everywhere. The crimped nylon bristles do an amazing job of getting it up and off upholstered furniture, bedding, car interiors, carpeting, and clothing. Available only from The Cleaning Center.

To receive a catalog with these and other great professional cleaning products, send a **postcard** with your name and address to:

> Clean Report
> P.O. Box 700
> Pocatello, ID 83204.

Full details on these and the whole universe of professional cleaning products can be found in *The Cleaning Encyclopedia* and *Is There Life After Housework?*

WHAT PAGE CAN I FIND IT ON?

... AND WHAT WERE THE
QUESTIONS AGAIN?

WHY DO YOU CARRY A
TOILET SUITCASE?

Doctors carry little black bags; lawyers and business executives carry attaché cases; I carry a toilet suitcase because I'm a professional cleaner. The toilet, which I clean regularly (as do eight million other professional cleaners and fifty million homemakers), is a symbol of my trade. I carry it to dispel any doubt as to how I feel about my profession—I'm proud of it.

I'll admit, however, that when I meet a business contact and reach in my suitcase to get a business card, nobody will take it! And there's always a lot of suspense when it bumps out of the carousel chute at airports as people wait to see who will claim it.

Thirty-five years ago I started my cleaning career to pay for my college education. I put an ad in the local paper and homeowners began to call me. I shrank a few carpets and streaked some walls and floors at first, but the homemakers whose homes I cleaned taught me as I went along. As I learned, I worked faster and developed new techniques for streamlining cleaning tasks—while still getting the job done right. I hired fellow students and named my growing company Varsity Contractors. Wanting to expand my business beyond homes, I landed a contract to clean the Bell Telephone building in our town—a big account! Today, Varsity Contractors is a multimillion dollar business with offices in sixteen states.

Not forgetting where I got my start, it was only

EAU CLAIRE DISTRICT LIBRARY

natural that I try to repay the wonderful homemakers who taught me the basics of cleaning. So I began giving seminars to women's groups across the country, showing them how to use professional cleaning products and techniques to save up to 75% of the time they now spent on housework. I also wanted to help homemakers be as proud of their profession as they should be.

I've been nicknamed by the media: "The Porcelain Preacher," "The Billy Graham of the Pine-Sol Set," "King of the Toilet Ring," "The Urinal Colonel," "Fastest Bowl Brush in the West," and "The Pied Piper of Purification." But I have the last laugh as I watch other businessmen trying to balance attaché cases, coats, and umbrellas while trying to read their *Wall Street Journals*. I just sit on my toilet suitcase and read my *Wall Street Journal*!

Don A. Aslett

For FREE information on:

☐ How to order professional cleaning supplies
☐ How to sponsor a Don Aslett Housecleaning Seminar/Workshop or speaking engagement in your area
☐ Don Aslett's schedule of appearances

Contact:
Don Aslett
P.O. Box 39
Pocatello, ID 83204